BRUTALLY HONEST WHILE HEARTWARMINGLY aligned with God, nature, and maternal mindfulness, *Walking the Labyrinth of My Heart*, takes us on a journey of faith, grief, and hope. Shortly after discovering that she is pregnant with her second child, Dianna receives a prenatal diagnosis of a lethal anomaly that sends her recently balanced world into a tailspin. We watch and root for her as she goes from disbelief, to recognition, to enlightenment. Through insightful journal entries, emails, poetry, and reflections, we see the progress of a pregnancy, the fate of which is largely beyond the author's control. As a result, Dianna becomes a fierce advocate for the few decisions that are within her control with the most important one being the ability to birth at home. The story is dynamic and open-ended as we experience with Dianna the penetrating pain of the pregnancy and the raw grief that follows the death shortly after birth of her much longed for daughter, *Mary Rose*. Dianna's transformation from brokenness to wholeness, from suffering to healing, "turning pain into Light and Love" is a witness to the impact of one tiny baby girl and to the path that they both traveled writing their story together.

Walking the Labyrinth of My Heart is a heart-wrenching but hopeful, even joyful journey, that searches for the symbolism that is apparent everywhere if only you open the eyes of your soul to unexpected miracles. This is a deeply moving and spiritual testament to the beauty of unconditional love. It is a must read for anyone who believes or wants to believe that there is a purpose to every life and that priceless mosaics begin with shards of broken glass.

Nancy Mayer-Whittington
Co-founder of Isaiah's Promise, Author of *For the Love of Angela*

This deeply emotional, heart-filled book could only have been written by a mother who has gone through the loss of her baby. This is a jewel of a book that can help other mothers walk this difficult path. May this book help them in their pain.

Jan Tritten, Editor and Founder of *Midwifery Today*

Dianna Vagianos Armentrout writes with the eloquence of a poet and the empathy of a grieving mother. This is a book for all bereaved parents, especially those who come to realize, while the baby is still in the womb, that fatality may occur. If you've lost a child, you'll find yourself gifted with techniques and information to help you through the deepest anguish into a fulfilled life. Moreover it's a must-read for anyone caring for and loving families who mourn for their children in the spirit world. *Walking the Labyrinth of my Heart* will sear your heart and inspire your spirit.

Terry Jones-Brady, Author of *A Mosaic Heart: Reshaping the Shards of a Shattered Life*

Dianna's journey of carrying a child most certainly destined for death, becomes uncharacteristically, a beautiful story of hope and faith. Highly recommended for any mother who has lost a child, this book is inspiring for anyone who has grieved a loved one. Instead of sadness, the reader walks away with a renewed appreciation for the precious gift of life.

Mary Potter Kenyon, author of five books,
including the award-winning *Refined by Fire: A Journey of Grief and Grace*

Walking the Labyrinth of My Heart is a much needed chronicle that will break open every woman's heart as Dianna shares her journey of carrying a beautiful baby, Mary Rose, diagnosed with trisomy 18 to term. It is a journey of pathos, loss, pain, and most of all, love. It is time to shatter the silence that women have borne far too long alone with mixed messages from the community regarding miscarriage, infertility, stillbirth and infant death. Dianna's journey is a spiritual one, and her words will serve as a comforting companion to many women who walk this path alone. Her words ring true: "We take our broken parts and carry them with our pain and walk on until we transmute that pain. Spring does come again no matter how cold the winter might be."

Sherry Reiter, PhD, LCSW, Director of The Creative Righting Center

With *Walking the Labyrinth of My Heart: A Journey of Pregnancy, Grief and Newborn Death,* Dianna gifts us with a book that leads straight into a piercing and necessary truth about death, grief, and life after. She takes us through the process of "finding her footing in the thick molasses of grief" in the same circular way grief took hold of her life. We labor with her through a willed pregnancy after being given the fatal diagnosis. Dianna helps us see that grief when juxtaposed with life creates an opening into our depths. She takes us through her pain with the elegance of someone who has looked into the heart of God, and knows that she is not alone.

Dianna eloquently blends her skills as writer, poetry therapist, researcher, and poet to show us the body of what I would call transcended grief. Dianna's spiritual growth deeply informs her writing and leads us into her world where little Mary Rose keeps blossoming beyond death. This book bursts with creative energy and pain all at once. More than merely expressing her grief, Dianna has written a forceful manifesto for claiming life in the face of pain, death and tragedy. One cannot but be changed by it.

Marianela Medrano, PhD, Author of *Goddesses of the Yuca*

All grief is a meditation on the unexplainable. Mourning a newborn daughter, after gestating a baby you know won't live, is beyond language and understanding. In fact it's almost beyond breathing. *Walking the Labyrinth of My Heart,* Dianna Vagianos Armentrout's powerful book, explores the excruciating depths of loss in a tone of elegiac prayerfulness. Perhaps prayerful contemplation is the only hope to find one's way in the swirling chaos of this kind of loss. We have no choice but to accept death and mourning, but in our hearts we never agree to it. Dianna's beautiful book, through language and love brings us along this unendurable pathway to as much comprehension as is possible.

Joanna Clapps Herman, Writer of *No Longer and Not Yet*
and *Anarchist Bastard: Growing up Italian in America*

Dianna Vagianos Armentrout's memoir is one parent's account of receiving a Trisomy 18 prenatal diagnosis for a much-wanted child. She shares how to navigate the necessary medical arrangements when there is a life-limiting condition, and addresses common obstacles that families encounter during the prelude and aftermath of Trisomy 18 deliveries. What makes Dianna's story especially compelling is the unique blend of religious and spiritual traditions, poetry and readings that guide her through her pregnancy, birth and the grief journey that follows.

Victoria J. Miller, Executive Director, Trisomy 18 Foundation

The stories that we tell the families who experience the early death of a child are in need of shifting. Dianna, a mother who herself experienced the death of a child, creates a context of change around how we relate to parents burying their children, and what it means to carry a child with a fatal illness to term instead of terminating the pregnancy. Her book stirs the soul to look at life and death from a culturally different perspective. Dianna invites us to re-examine our entire worldview about life itself and faith, and the way we speak to others about their own experiences of life and death. She also shows us that in the telling one's own story there is healing, even when the child's life is a brief flash of light.

Shiloh Sophia McCloud, Artist, Co-founder of Intentional Creativity

Nothing could have prepared Dianna Vagianos Armentrout for the multifaceted and deeply painful experience of losing her newborn baby. Her story, honest, emotional and at times raw, stimulates one's own memory of pain, *Walking the Labyrinth of My Heart* is a courageous memoir guiding the reader on a personal journey through the many stages of grief. While the devastation she feels is palpable, the love for her child and continued connection to her beautiful spirit shines through each page. Her poignant insights into the message of loss reveal an opportunity to heal and the chance to mend a broken heart. There are many tragedies in life; this one created a book reminding us of how precious life is, no matter how short it might be.

Elizabeth Harper, Color Intuitive, Artist, Author of
Wishing: How to Fulfill Your Heart's Desires and *365 Days of Angel Prayers*
www.sealedwithlove.com

This is a searing and wise telling of one woman's journey through the most difficult landscapes of faith and grief. Dianna Vagianos Armentrout writes with such honest and tender sadness that her words eventually merge with light. The story of the birth and death of Mary Rose will stay with me for a very long time.

Amy Wright Glenn, Author of
Birth, Breath, and Death: Meditations on Motherhood, Chaplaincy and Life as a Doula

Dianna is our spiritual midwife. She teaches us how to create the space for a profound grace to emerge between us, for fragility, wisdom, and quietness in the face of the unimaginable. In taking us with her on this unfathomable journey of grief, mourning the loss of her newborn daughter, she opens our hearts and leads us to "so august a station."

Aniela Costello, Licensed Homeopathic Practitioner
Lecturer, Homeopathic Concepts LLC

"I insisted on making my own way through a system that doesn't offer many choices." "Mary Rose focused me, broke me open to love more. . . . In our tiny fragment of time together, there was profound truth and mercy." In Dianna's *Walking the Labyrinth of My Heart*, the glaring hypocrisies and platitudes of society, religion and culture toward parenting, pregnancy, infant death and grief are all observed in such an honest and provocative way, that one does not merely read this book, but experiences it, and is left captivated, wounded, marveled for the treachery that is the bereaved parent's sojourn. That we have established a universal and systematic sterilization of grief is pointedly called out, time and again, and evaluated through a raw candor and impossible wisdom. Such a writing is divinely inspired, a balm and real hope for any bereaved mother's heart, and is quite frankly a necessary guidepost of observations and lessons for every member of society. We have been parched for such truth; we have been in danger without it. I am a bereaved mother, and if you consider yourself part of my village, my community, my society, I must ask that you read and heed the value of Dianna's journey.

Heidi Faith, *still*birthday founder

Dianna Vagianos Armentrout's unforgettable debut book, *Walking the Labyrinth of My Heart*, firmly establishes her as a master of courage and faith. Her deeply felt passages leap off the page and into the reader's heart. Like any great artist, she turns her human experiences into a work of art that is soul searching, honest and powerfully moving.

The poet's strong female voice rises above the grief of carrying to term a child she knows will not live long and illuminates the "raw and holy" one-hour they shared in this physical world together. She lines her path, through the labyrinth of anguish and heartache, with roses, fully knowing her heart will be punctured by thorns. She is the holy chalice at the center of this labyrinth brimming with unconstrained truth and sorrow yet joyous and thankful for the cadre of women who supported and surrounded her with love.

With the exquisite showcase of talent displayed in this book honoring Mary Rose, the author celebrates her daughter's life, no matter how short, with the certain knowledge that love never dies.

Dianalee Velie, Author of four poetry books, including *The Alchemy of Desire*

A powerful book that shares wisdom and comfort, love and beauty as it confronts the most unimaginable of losses. I have long admired Dianna Vagianos Armentrout as a poet and poetry therapist. Here she invites us to walk beside her on the labyrinthine path of a mother's grief. Here her great heart, soul, intelligence, spirit, prayer and poetry bring light to darkness and healing to suffering.

Judith Baumel, Poet and Founding Director of Creative Writing at Adelphi University

Walking the Labyrinth of My Heart

A Journey of Pregnancy, Grief and Newborn Death

BY DIANNA VAGIANOS ARMENTROUT

June 2019

To Lorane,

For the healing
of all women.

With Love +
Respect for your work,

Love,

Dianna

ISBN: 978-0-9821176-4-4 (paperback)
978-0-9821176-5-1 (ebook)

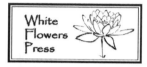

White Flowers Press

© 2016

for Mary Rose

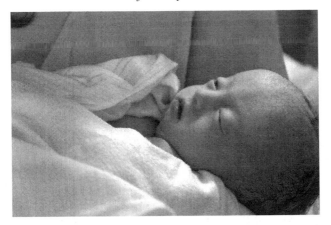

She rose up into the shadowing mercy of God
and was plunged in an ocean of light. Unto her
be salutations and praise, compassion and glory.
May God make sweet her resting place
with the outpourings of His heavenly mercy.
Bahá'i prayer

Table of Contents

Preface

MY BABY IS DEAD. For five months of my pregnancy I knew that my daughter, Mary Rose, would die, though I did not know when she would die. What surprises me most is that I am alive. I am alive after the heartache of knowing about her condition, alive after holding her still body in my arms moments after her birth. Afterpains came with empty arms, as did my baby's milk. Those months of pregnancy with the knowledge that our baby had trisomy 18 felt like a million years of sadness. Yet things change. As I approach the second anniversary of her birth and death, it is springtime and everywhere I look there are pregnant women and healthy babies. Time is moving quickly again, and I am catching up.

During my pregnancy I did not find much to comfort me. I am writing the book that I wish I could have read when I was pregnant with my daughter. When parents find out that their unborn baby has anomalies, they want answers. The medical community does not have all the answers to our questions, even as we undergo tests and come closer to the truth. Our mid-pregnancy ultrasound revealed that our daughter most likely had trisomy 18 or 13. I was 42 years old and there was talk about my "advanced" age. However, most babies with trisomies are born to mothers younger than 35. Mary Rose had cysts on her brain and a heart defect. She measured small and her hands were folded in the way of babies with trisomy 18. The best hope that the doctor could offer was that she would have Down syndrome and a heart defect. I now know that parents in our situation sometimes pray for a child with Down syndrome. Babies with Down syndrome live.

From the moment of the ultrasound, I entered a medical world that most pregnant women do not know exists. I learned the language of trisomy 18 and fatal diagnoses. I stopped answering my phone, and I looked around in sadness. My two-year-old son kissed my swelling belly, and I wept. My eyes were perpetually brimming with tears. My husband and I chose to carry our daughter to term. The life that God gave her would have to be enough for us.

We negotiated our reality the best that we could. We planned a funeral while pregnant, and we tried to prepare for the grief that would come later, while we mourned our pregnancy outcomes. There were not enough therapy hours to prepare me for the death of my baby. I was shocked when the pregnancy was over, when my daughter, who barely breathed, died. In the months that followed I had to find my footing in the thick molasses of grief. As I attempted to reenter "normal" life, I went to church and faced pregnant women and living newborns. I walked slowly in grocery stores while people rushed around me. It took me months to be able to speak to friends on the phone without weeping. Why doesn't the world pause just for a moment after our lives are shattered by illness and death and grief?

It is very difficult to live with pregnancy and infant loss in our hyper-electronic, fast-paced, death-fearing American culture. I'm not sure how it is in other countries, though my family in Greece integrates death and tragedy in daily conversation. In this country there is not much space for those grieving babies and pregnancies. We hear, *You can have another,* and, *Aren't you over that yet?* People do not mention our babies. They do not speak their names. How do we understand juxtapositions like infant/death, mis/carriage, still/birth? Yet we walk at the crossroads between life and death when we deal with pregnancy and infant loss. Thankfully there are many online communities that meet some of our needs after a fatal diagnosis, but there is little support in our day-to-day life as we continue our lives without our babies. Sometimes people offer comfort initially, but not consistently through the months and years of our grief.

It is my intention and hope that this book comforts parents going through pregnancy and infant loss, particularly those whose pregnancy dreams have been shattered by medical news. Many people bury their children at different ages and stages of life. A pregnancy with the knowledge of death is a challenge that is worthy of further exploration. People say, *I know how you feel,* but I truly know. I have walked this path, and I hope that I can be of service and comfort to others by writing about my experience and grief process. In writing about Mary Rose, I pray that her own life continues to touch others. She is our intercessor and helps in the way that ancestors help. As an intercessor, Mary Rose prays and intervenes on our behalf. She protects our living children.

I will clarify three points here.

1. An ultrasound and bloodwork told us that Mary Rose had trisomy 18, but she could not technically be diagnosed until she was born. Once born, she would exist in the medical system, but not before. I often use "diagnosis" to indicate this in my essays and on my blog, but I will forgo the quotation marks in this text.

2. Some neonatal illnesses have a range of possibilities in terms of life expectancy and the baby's functionality. Our daughter could have been born still. She could have lived a few minutes or hours or days. Approximately 8% of babies born with trisomy 18 make it to their first birthdays. There are very few people with trisomy 18 living into adulthood. No one knows why some live longer. I refer to this range often because it was hard to prepare for Mary Rose's birth with so many possibilities.

3. In order to protect the two midwives present at Mary Rose's birth, I have changed their names. An anonymous medical complaint was filed a year after Mary Rose's birth and death, and an investigation followed.

I see life as a spiritual path. I can only make sense of Mary Rose's life if I look at it from a distance. I put myself in the context of my grandmothers and great-grandmothers. Women have been burying their children since the beginning of time. I am one woman who has walked this searing path of pain. Yet somewhere inside our hearts we have the strength to carry on, not to move on, as some would want us to do. We can continue our lives, taking our babies with us. Our arms are empty, but our hearts are full. The love that we have for our children, living or dead, grows. I do not believe in a final good-bye.

I am comforted by the thought that Mary Rose is beside me as I write, urging me on. Her soul has a purpose. Her body was the body she needed to do her soul's work. I know that my daughter comforts people. I know that she prays. It is with this knowledge that I wake up each morning knowing that my two children were destined to be my son and my daughter. I bless them both as I step into each day and set the kettle to boil for another cup of tea.

Part I

Pregnancy Journal and Emails

. . . The way she must have had everything she wanted in the womb, without asking. . . .

Denise Duhamel

March 20, 2014

It is springtime, and even here in Hampton Roads, Virginia, the winter was difficult. I am five months pregnant and just found out that my baby has trisomy 18, a fatal illness. *It's totally random,* the genetic counselor said. *Only 2–3% of pregnancies at your advanced maternal age are affected.* Daffodils mock me as the weather warms.

I am not terminating my pregnancy because my baby lives and moves inside me. I'm not functioning well. My two-year-old son gets me through the days, but I can't help crying. My friends call, but I don't answer the phone. People send me emails, but I don't respond to most of them. Ninety-two percent of these babies die before their first birthday. Fifty percent before or during labor. I'm not growing like I did with my first pregnancy. I'm mad when I look in the mirror. People have complimented me on not gaining too much weight. Then when I start to grow a little, I get mad some more. I wonder how my dying baby is growing. It hasn't even been two weeks since we found out.

How can my body nurture this baby only for it to die? It has a heart defect, cysts on the brain, and a few other markers. It might be deformed. Some of these babies have cleft lips and eyes that are spaced differently. Boys usually die before birth. Girls live longer. My mother has been praying for me to have a daughter. How cliché to want the earth to swallow me whole, to cover me up in my pain and bury me. I have to think about a baby coffin and a cemetery plot. I was thinking the only thing that I would need is a double stroller. And that first outfit? Will my sick baby live or will I bury my baby in its first dress?

We are cracked open by our pain and by our circumstances. The Light comes through. I get it. I've facilitated workshops about illness and grief, but laboring and burying a baby never entered my mind, though if I'm honest I've always been afraid of having a stillbirth. My friend Miko reminded me yesterday that I was terrified of this ultrasound. *You didn't say something was wrong, but it was like you knew,* she said. I was sick to my stomach upon entering the hospital for the test.

Flowers arrive from friends today. I thought that they would cheer me, but they make me sadder. Springtime makes me sadder. Doctors' offices make me sadder. Church services also set me back emotionally. There are healthy pregnant women everywhere and beautiful healthy newborns sitting in their car seats cooing.

My son stops several times a day to give me extra kisses. He knows something is wrong, and he cries when he hears me crying. I stay busy doing truck puzzles and playing with him. He has a silly, hearty laugh. I am grateful for this joy. I am grateful that this is not my first pregnancy. But my heart is heavy.

March 22 (Email Update to Family and Friends)

Good morning,

I am writing to sum up our visit yesterday with the midwife. Tim says that he didn't think that we could get any sadder, yet with each step, we do.

Grace, the midwife, came to the house to examine me and went into detail about trisomy 18. She explained that it is an illness of the central line of the body, hence the brain and heart defects. Often (though mostly with trisomy 13, another fatal illness) the baby has a cleft lip – also central line. She explained that because of the brain's lack of development, these babies often cannot suck. We will have to decide if we will put a feeding tube in our newborn, should it be born alive.

If I go into labor before 36 weeks, she expects the baby to be stillborn. After 36 weeks she expects the baby to live through labor, and then we might have a few minutes, hours or days. It is also expected that labor will be normal. Grace does not anticipate any complications at this point. She does not think that I will need a C-section. Most likely the baby will be smaller, between 5 and 6.5 pounds.

If we do not get on board with "heroic measures," such as the feeding tube and heart surgery, she does not expect the baby to live long (and even with intervention, we are looking at a few months, since most do not make it to their first birthday). Right now Tim and I do not want artificial means of keeping the baby alive. My baby cannot be cured. There is a small chance that it will have partial or mosaic trisomy 18, which is a milder illness. Grace said that if the baby is born and looks healthier than we expect, then we can change our minds about the interventions.

Tim insists that I birth in a hospital. We will visit an ob/gyn at least once to make our birth plans known in the chart, then go to a neonatologist to make our plan for no interventions and get a Do Not Resuscitate Order (DNR). The midwife suggests that we preregister the baby with neonatal hospice. I did not know that such a thing existed. She also suggested that I hire a bereavement doula to support me during labor, but also to help with some practicalities like shopping. Will we need diapers? Baby clothes?

Grace came with books called *When Hello Means Good-Bye* and *We Were Gonna Have a Baby, But We Had an Angel Instead*. Depressing and sad. Tim didn't stay with us for most of the visit. He has a hard time dealing with the details of the death of his child.

Father John gave me the name of an Orthodox coffin maker. I contacted him and I now have an email titled "Yes We Can Provide a Coffin for Your Sweet Baby" that I cannot bring myself to answer. We will have the funeral at our parish and then bury the baby nearby.

If the baby dies in my womb, I will have a choice to labor at home. The midwife says that we will know ahead of time and can make that decision if we get there.

Thank you for your love and support.

Dianna

March 24

I miss my unborn baby already. Yesterday in church the parish sang "God grant you many years" for a child's name day. It was a reminder that we'll miss birthdays and Christmases and many other things. Crawling and walking and talking. I miss a lifetime of milestones already. First day of school and graduation. Smiling and laughing. Holding hands.

March 27

For about four seconds I was jealous of my sister and her two healthy children. My two-year old niece was screaming, *Brother, brother, brother.* I almost cried thinking about how I want my son to be a big brother to a living sibling. We find out the sex of our baby in four days. Will my son have a brother or sister?

March 31

It's a girl.

April 1

Mary Rose

April 5

This week has been long and difficult. I feel Mary Rose moving inside me, but I want to hold her and feed her and smell her hair. Her defects are in the brain and heart. Does that mean that she can live longer than other babies who have more defects? Do I want to bury a newborn? Do I want a sick baby for months or years (though I know that years are unlikely)? Waiting for appointments with the neonatologist and the pediatric cardiologist. I want to know how long my baby will live without heart surgery. I want to know how I will handle postpartum healing when my milk comes in. I want to know if my baby will suck or breathe on her own. I want to understand why this is happening. Why do I still see a healthy baby in our house growing up with our son?

I sat on the grass outside today and put both hands on the Earth Mother. I felt her truth rise up like a spiral reminding me gently that not all life is meant to live long and thrive. *Some go soon into the earth and bear much fruit,* I heard in my heart center. My tiny girl. My little one will become one with the earth and feed others. I am hungry for different circumstances. I am never un-sad anymore.

April 6

We say that we are expecting when we are pregnant and fertile, abundantly creating new life. When I was pregnant with my son, I eagerly anticipated meeting my boy. I wanted to hold him and know him. Smell him and hold his little hands. Kiss his feet. I am 15 weeks away from my due date with my daughter, and I understand expecting differently this time. I feel like I am holding life and death in my body, but my body wants only life and nurturing. I want to nest, but there is nothing to nest. Today I ordered my baby's coffin, and though I hope she doesn't use it, I see it in front of me. Our path.

When I was pregnant with my son, my aunt was dying of recurring irregular meningioma. A shaman and esoteric astrologer told me that I was helping to birth her to the other side while I was birthing my son into this world. After he was born we visited her often. I would prop him up on her hospital bed between her legs that were swollen from fluid and steroids, and at first she could move her right arm and touch him. She could place her right index finger to her mouth and make silly noises to make him laugh. As he grew and moved his hands, then held toys, she regressed, barely able to use that right arm. I was watching this ironic juxtaposition, these two people's paths unfolding before me. She died when my son was 16 months old, fighting her illness day and night. He was *her* boy and she lived for him, adored him. *How can I let go of you and your son and your mother?* she asked me more than once.

How can I let go of my infant daughter? Have I ever cried as much as now? Even through a difficult divorce after 15 years of marriage to a mentally ill man? Even after mourning my aunt's death more than I thought possible? (Weren't we mourning her for four years as she deteriorated?) I feel this threshold of life and death in my womb. My child is walking the worlds as she grows and moves inside me. I imagine that I will have a lovely rose garden for her when Tim and I buy a house. I see her ever before me, but always this baby, this tiny life that has already touched so many. Her brain and heart are damaged, yet I know that her soul is intact. She is now my teacher.

My Qigong teacher told me to let go of all expectations. But I am expecting. Life or death. It will be one or the other. I do not know if we will bring our daughter home, or if we do, for how long. I do not know how many outfits to buy her, although I understand that one will be a burial dress. I am pregnant and my womb grows. I think of Mary, her womb holding God. Aren't all children holy? *Help me, Mother Mary, to walk this path.* The road is neither straight nor paved.

April 8

I thought that I was coming to terms with things, but I broke down and wept for almost half an hour uncontrollably. I couldn't stop until I took a grief remedy. I don't want to give my baby to God. I don't want to lose my daughter. I want my healthy daughter and her life here with me. This feels like a cruel trick. Crueler than a psychotic first husband or a cat that dies of brain tumors while my aunt is diagnosed with hers. I don't think that I will ever recover from this loss. And today Mary Rose is moving so much. She dances around, getting more active each day. I wonder if I'll miss her even more when she is born and out of my body since this is the most time I'll have with her.

I bought a small package of newborn diapers today for Mary Rose from Target, and then when I got in the car "You are My Sunshine" came on the radio. "Please don't take my sunshine away." I wanted to look at the girls' dresses, but I walked on, pushing the cart while my son sat and held his red Spider-Man toothbrush. I tried to keep my eyes straight ahead instead of looking down the aisles. It is time to try to sleep. The darkness means more these days.

April 9

It is late and I'm up. Baking peanut butter cookies, emptying the dishwasher, sweeping. I'm exhausted. I have a headache from crying so much last night. Somewhere in all of this motion, I realize I don't want to go upstairs and sleep because that brings me one day closer to burying my daughter.

April 10

I am walking in a world of contradictions. My baby is moving and growing inside my womb. She is growing to die. Her heartbeat sounds strong, but her heart is broken and defective. She is safe in my body where I can breathe and eat for her, but once she is born she will not be able to survive for long, let alone thrive. I am pregnant and abundant, but when my body is healing from labor I will not have a baby to feed and nurture. I have a son and I will bury a daughter. This pregnancy feels like a cruel prison sentence. I often want it to be over, yet each day brings me closer to burying my child. I don't think I will ever have the strength to live through my baby's funeral service. We can keep our baby alive with feeding tubes and oxygen or we can let her die a natural death. Is this the threshold that poets speak of? This doorway between one world and the next? The place where my aunt waited a long time before she finally stepped through?

I received a package from a kind, well-meaning friend with some words about positive thoughts to heal the baby. It depressed me. All this talk about positive thinking. . . . Does it imply that negative thoughts create chromosomal disorders? If I could heal my daughter with thoughts, wouldn't I? Why are humans so obstinate when it comes to death and illness? We deny their place in life. We believe that juicing and cleansing and meditating can cure all ills, but we live in a fallen world. There is sickness around us. People die. I don't see this as a battle that I can win. We have a limited amount of time on the planet, and then we move on. I am working toward accepting Mary Rose's fatal illness and summoning the courage to let her go. I'm certain that I didn't give her this disease. I'm certain that God has the power to heal her, if He wills it. But as the mother carrying this child, I feel that her life will be brief. I see the coffin before us, the ground to lay her in.

Sometimes I think that this is all a mistake, that my baby is fine, but this lasts for a few seconds. Mostly I think of Mary the Mother of God and her words "Be it unto me according to Thy word" (King James Bible, Luke 1:38). I am powerless even as the creator of this child, even as her mother. And I will be in this place of thresholds for some time. I straddle the contradictions of a pregnancy that will end in death in my heart center and body, working toward a deepening understanding of life. Humans want to believe that things will always be okay. Only the reality of the current breath is real. It is time to rein in all my expectations and be grateful for the beauty of this present moment. Husband, son, daughter. My family. I am loved and I love.

I went outside this afternoon and heard things I usually don't hear: a woodpecker and other birds, leaves falling onto the driveway, the wind itself blowing through the trees. I used to hear these things years ago when I was present, reading Thich Nhat Hanh's book *The Miracle of Mindfulness*, also going through a crisis: the ex-husband's psychotic breakdown. I was 28. My homeopath explained that every seven years, according to Chinese medicine, we go through a crisis. *Your body is completely new every seven years*, she said. *That is how long it takes to make completely new cells.* It was the year 2000. I am now about to turn 42, another crisis year.

Something has been bothering me. The mothers in the grief books say that the rest of the pregnancy is time with the baby. They say that it is good to go on outings to spend time with the baby before it dies, but I don't agree. Is going to the zoo now the same as taking a growing baby to the zoo? Right now Tim is tickling our son, who is laughing, and I wish that Mary Rose could one day experience such joy and love. But she won't, and pretending that I'm taking her to the zoo when I can't hear her squeals of laughter does me a disservice as a grieving mother. I do think that I will look back on this pregnancy and miss the feeling of fullness, of knowing my child is growing inside me, but it is bittersweet. I am overwhelmed by the complexities of my emotions and thoughts. Losing her won't be easy, but then I will be able to move forward to some degree, to put this pregnancy behind me, to grieve fully without the movements that remind me that life is so tentative and unfair, so fragile. This takes me back to that feeling of this pregnancy as a prison sentence. There is not even a second of a break for me. I cannot forget about the baby at work or in the shower, as my husband can. She is part of me and right now we are one. Mother and child. One.

April 13

I'm so tired my eyes burn. I've been cleaning because I'm upset. I cooked for hours today until I had muscle spasms going down my legs. How will I live through 14 more weeks of this anticipation? I've thought, *Stop it*, a few times as Mary Rose kicked, then felt so much guilt. I pray every night to St. Anthimos to take this child up to Mother Mary, to heal her completely and bring her to the heavenly worlds. And then yesterday I started praying that I deliver sooner. What kind of mother wants her child out of her body, wishes her to stop moving, to stop reminding her of the reality of the situation? What kind of mother prays that her child will die? I do. I pray not only because I don't want her to suffer, but because of my own selfishness. I do not want to be tied down to taking care of a sick child for decades. So much shadow inside myself. . . .

April 27

I spoke to Nancy Eagle Spirit Woman a couple of days ago. She is a shaman and had told me to believe in a miracle for my current pregnancy. She said, *If you don't believe, how can a miracle happen?* But I knew even then that my baby would not stay on this earth. I had not spoken to Nancy in a few weeks, but I sent her a letter to pray for me to have the strength to let Mary Rose go. I shared the message I felt from Mary Rose's soul: she came to cleanse the ancestral lines for both my family and Tim's family. My messages have been that this pregnancy is about love. Nancy connected with her guides and told me, *It is an honor for you to carry this baby and love her and give her life so that she can cross over to heaven so young. You have been chosen by Spirit to carry her. She needs love, and you and Tim and her brother are giving her that love. Don't let her go with grief and sadness, let her go with JOY! And she will always be with you, and she will help you write.*

April 28

Yesterday I told my son that we are naming our baby after Mary, and that she is going to go to heaven to be with Jesus. He touched my leg tenderly and said, *Your son is staying with Mommy.*

April 30

Sindy brings me the painting, "Healing Companion," on a rainy afternoon. When I step into the living room to see her work, I am in awe of the energy. I have 14 weeks of pregnancy left, and I briefly contemplated throwing myself down one of the steep ravines in our neighborhood. It was only for a moment as I walked with my son in the stroller, showing him the lily of the valley and other springtime flowers. *That would take care of the pregnancy and me,* I thought. But after seeing the painting, I believe that I can survive this pregnancy. I now feel shored up with energy and love.

I sit under the painting often, sometimes with my son who exclaims, *It's beautiful!* I feel the strength and love of the mother, the child angel holding her with such tenderness. For now I know that I will make it through this difficult time, accepting the outcomes as they are, believing in the miracle of loving through this, and not praying for a perfectly healthy baby when that is not Mary Rose's path.

May 4

Dear God,

I think you have lost your God-mind. I can't do this after everything I have been through these past couple of decades. I cannot labor only to have my newborn baby die. And when are you going to tell me what will happen? Stillborn. A few hours. A few days. Weeks? Months? I feel like this is a cruel fate. How can I get through it? I am getting a few clothes together and it is painful. A ruffled yellow dress. Newborn undershirts and tiny pink socks. Will she see the outside? Will she meet her grandparents or aunt or cousins? Eleven more weeks and each day continues to bring more tears, more anguish. Three difficult appointments coming up: cardiologist, neonatologist, pediatric hospice. They are insurmountable mountains in front of me that I must climb. What a test. I want to rail against you. It's not fair! It's not fair! We have so much love in this family. Why this? Why? When you give healthy babies to sick people. Crackheads and addicts, alcoholics and mentally unstable people. Who am I to judge? I judge myself most. I feel inadequate to make the decisions at hand, especially when Tim has a hard time talking about all of this. You will be carrying me for a long time, God. I'm too weary to go on.

June 27

> I build a lighted house and there indwell. *Mantra, Sign of Cancer*

I built a sacred house carefully, slowly, to birth my baby of Light at home, and it has been pillaged. I am nearly 37 weeks pregnant, and I squat in the rubble of my labors unable to know what to do next. My dress is torn, my hair is wild. I am a mother who has been told I don't know what is best for my child, though I have carried her after being offered a termination. Even here sifting through the remains of my house and birth plan, I don't want to go to the hospital. Why can't I birth my baby outside the system? Why do people work to manipulate others, leaving broken walls and shattered windows behind them?

It took a long time to come to the birth plan of laboring at home. My daughter has trisomy 18, and it took doctors' visits and discussions and a clearer understanding of the range of her life expectancy to figure out a way home. After a few doctors gave us permission for a home birth, I thought that the way would be clear.

My baby will die. I will hold a dead baby in my arms and weep, and society can't accept this as part of the messiness of life. Dead babies belong in hospitals and morgues, not at home surrounded peacefully by love with no machines and no intrusions. A funeral home is needed. Doctors are needed to measure her and confirm the pregnancy screenings which are close to 99% accurate. After almost four months of dealing with the reality that I'm carrying a child who won't live long, who is too sick to function with us, making decisions about not wanting life support, feeling trapped in a body with my sweet baby and these hormones that urge me to nest while I plan a burial, I am paralyzed by shock. In the muck that has become my life, my fingers are dirty with mud and water.

Our systems are based on fear. A hospice nurse manager who was supposed to make this process of preparing for a fatally ill child smooth and easy, worked behind the scenes expressing her fears and manipulating others. She actually held the DNR until I said that I would birth in the hospital. But I've changed my mind. I feel bullied. I feel angry, but I don't want to spend the rest of my pregnancy in this energy. The nurse doesn't think that home birth is safe. The nurse is afraid that Mary Rose might have trouble breathing and suffer. The nurse wants morphine in the house. The nurse believes that I want my daughter to die sooner because I do not want a feeding tube on a four-pound baby. The nurse worked hard behind the scenes and then showed her cheerful face at my door yesterday to deliver the DNR.

Even in this rubble I will stand in the light and walk away from fear. Death is not bad and life good. We birth little ones into living, and we birth those leaving this world into the next. I am standing on a threshold of the worlds, and I will keep sacred my daughter's unique path. She is loved from both sides of the veil.

July 2

I spent my birthday cleaning shit, literally. I am 42 years old and my two-year old son has the worst diarrhea of his life. I started out thinking that I would go out to lunch with a friend, but yesterday sciatica set in so that I could barely walk. I have a good husband, a healthy son, a pregnancy with a sweet baby girl who will pass away, but who has filled me up with love. I am limping and my son is exhausted and sick, but it's still my birthday. I find two chocolate cupcakes in the freezer. My husband brings me a hot dog with a candle in it. There is no going out, no date night, no chocolate mousse pie, just shit. But we are in this together.

Last week brought on the unraveling of my birth plan for a home birth due to an over-zealous and manipulative hospice nurse. I wept and railed against the unfairness of it all, especially the added stress to an already stressful pregnancy so close to my due date. I believe that we have a pediatrician who will come to the house when she returns from her vacation on July 14. But what if Mary Rose comes sooner? We have no plan until then except for the hospital. Grace suggests that I call the pediatric cardiologist one more time to see if he can help us with a diagnosis when Mary Rose is born. He has cleared us for home birth and written a letter of support. I call today and he calls me back. He keeps repeating, *I don't understand what the problem is. Why can't you take her to the pediatrician for a diagnosis and not be in the hospital?* I tell him that it didn't seem like a problem initially, but that I believed the nurse had manipulated the situation and brought up legalities and fears. I tell him that I heard the word "manslaughter" if Mary Rose dies in the house. I tell him that the doctors are now saying that the baby has not been diagnosed. He replies, *What about all of these tests? Don't they count?* So this perplexed, kind cardiologist who clearly has respect for the parents of dying children, will confirm the diagnosis at his office after Mary Rose is born. If there is an investigation about her death should she die at home, he will call it off. So even in the middle of all of this shit and pain, there is hope and beauty.

I see a birthing pool under Sindy's painting where I can labor my precious angel under her image. I've been asked what my hang-up is with the hospital. I don't want to be in an institution for the precious short time I have with Mary Rose. I don't want to compromise. Most parents of healthy babies have their children's lives ahead of them in years and decades. Starting out in the hospital with a few tests is not such a big deal to them. Mary Rose might have hours or days. I want to hold my baby girl and let her know only love in her short life. I am hopeful that I'll get my wish after all, and that everything is happening for our highest good. I keep asking myself, *Will she wait for July 14th?* I'll find out soon enough. The actors in this play are lining up. My mother comes on July 5th, my sister and her family on the 10th, and then my father will join us.

When Tim and I finally settle into bed, we watch the last hour of *Moonstruck* on my broken computer. I'm lying down on my ice pack. I turn to him and say, *This is kind of romantic isn't it?* He replies, *In a pathetic way.* He kisses me. We laugh at the screen. This long day is finally over.

July 6

When my aunt was bedridden she would often say, *What am I going to do now?* and she said it in Greek, *Τι θα κάνω τώρα?* I didn't know how to answer her. Now I ask, *How am I going to do this? How am I going to labor only to let my baby die?* These questions are different. My aunt had a type A personality and needed control. She asked her aide, *Who's the boss here?* until she died. The former elementary school principal needed to know that she was still in control. I understand that I have to do something that I don't want to do, and my question is more a pleading with God and the Universe. *How? How do you expect me to walk this path?*

My leg pain is no better after a week. I have stretched and tried to relax. I can barely go up and down stairs. I am due in about two weeks, and I am convinced that the culmination of my own fears and the stress of dealing with hospice is the cause of this pain. It has been a year of stop and go, process and weep, move forward, cry some more, gather some strength, feel drained, imagine Light guiding it all. . . . It has been a year of shattered glasses and dishes, of awakened spiritual understanding, of writing about my pregnancy. It has been a year of comforting my toddler who doesn't want to leave my side.

I am not at my baby's funeral yet. I am not meeting her yet. Mary Rose is the greatest loss of my life, though I haven't lost her yet. I imagine her in the heavenly worlds with my paternal grandmother and Mary the Mother of God. I see her praying for us as an intercessor, a guardian for her brother and cousins. I see her in the future welcoming each of us as we walk through that threshold into the Light.

July 14

I figured out one thing late last night about this pain. I'm stuck because deep, deep down I know that when Mary Rose is born I won't be able to breathe or eat for her. So this labor is about letting go of my being able to care for my little girl with my body. And then there are all of the unknowns.

July 19

I got that happy hormone feeling last night. The one that says, *A baby is coming! You are going to meet your baby!* And perhaps because I took another high dose of ignatia for grief, I let myself feel it.

July 31, 2014 (Email to Therapist)

We are entering the season of the church for Mary, the *Theotokos* or God-bearer. Tomorrow starts the fast for her Dormition. The feast is on August 15, when we honor that Jesus came and took his mother up to heaven just as Elijah. No body to be buried as in Jesus, Elijah, and the Holy Mother.

Mary Rose feels large like an angel. I saw her last night rising up into the after-world from a tiny baby body, a shining, luminous, giant, bright light. I feel chosen somehow to bear this suffering, this life and death. The Mother presence is huge with this pregnancy. Even Mary's mother has drawn near. I've been singing her hymn in my head for months: "The barren woman gives birth to the *Theotokos*. . . ." How old was St. Anna when she birthed Holy Mary?

I have to surrender. I have to accept that Mary Rose's days are numbered and that this is for our highest good. I pray that she dies sooner after the cardiologist explained how the heart defect would take her. Her lungs would get too much blood and she would have trouble breathing. It could take a while, and I do not want my baby to suffer. The babies who die a few days after birth die peacefully and quietly, sleeping more and more until they leave their body.

I worry too that my body won't know how to go into labor given the trisomy 18 condition of the placenta. This too takes surrendering.

Here we are in Mother Mary's time of the year.

Part II
Essays and Blog Posts

This day only that which is for my Highest Good
shall come to me. Only that which is Light shall leave me.

Gloria Karpinski

The Baby Who Became a Seal

I STAND IN THE GIFT SHOP AT THE Virginia Aquarium in February, almost halfway through my second pregnancy looking for a small stuffed animal to set up an altar for my unborn child. I am scheduled for my first ultrasound the following week. I hold a blue dolphin in my hands and remember my first midwife, Vicki, and her nephew.

I interviewed Vicki before my son was born. I needed to figure out his birth after I moved to New York, and I wanted to birth him at home with a midwife. I asked Vicki if any of her babies had ever died. *Yes*, she said, *One baby. He was my nephew.* She told me that before he was born she had a dream that her nephew looked like a seal swimming in deep, dark waters. She told me that Ian, her nephew's older brother, asked his father, *What if the baby isn't a baby? What if the baby is a seal?* When the baby had low heart tones toward the end of the pregnancy, his mother, Karen, went to the hospital to deliver and, soon after labor, without any knowledge of his condition, he died as she held him.

I bought that small dolphin and put it by my bed. A few days later I found out that my baby had several anomalies and might have trisomy 18 or 13. *The best scenario is that this baby has Down syndrome and a heart defect*, the doctor said. When I trained recently to become a Peer Minister for Isaiah's Promise, the trainer from Be Not Afraid said, *Our parents pray for Down syndrome. Those babies live. Those babies are miracles when you have a fatal diagnosis.* I didn't pray for that particular trisomy because somehow I knew that the sadness I had felt, the sadness that I thought was exhaustion, might have been some intuitive knowing. My baby would be severely disabled. My baby would have no muscle tone. My baby would die.

I texted Vicki to tell her about my ultrasound results, and she told me then that her nephew, John Gilbert, died of trisomy 18. I imagine the baby swimming in deep water, his body lithe and dark. A sweet boy. Someone's son. A Light.

When pediatric hospice tried to sabotage my home birth, Vicki offered her home to me to birth Mary Rose peacefully. She had a friend in hospice and had already made contact with her. I felt so loved, surrounded by Grace here in my house with Vicki's support reaching from New Jersey to Virginia. I recently had tea with Vicki and she told me more about John Gilbert's birth. After John died, his mother decided to pump and donate her son's milk to other infants. His mother pumped for six weeks and, during that time, Vicki got calls from all over the tri-state area from mothers who needed breast milk for their infants. John's mother pumped gallons of milk, and Vicki drove that milk to the Bronx, to Westchester, Rockland County, around New Jersey. His milk fed five babies in that time. Vicki says, *John Gilbert continues to bless families by putting babies in need with extra milk years later. Whenever a mother donates milk, I get a call from someone who needs it.*

In Patricia Harman's novel *The Midwife of Hope River*, Mrs. Potts, an older midwife, is talking to the narrator, a younger midwife, about her son.

"Is he grown?"

"No, he died. Died at birth. . . ."

"That's what makes you a good midwife," the old lady says. "You know the value of life, and you know loss. My father used to say the two are one, like the bramble and the rose. Life and death . . . the bramble and the rose" (200).

John Gilbert and Mary Rose are integral parts of our lives. Vicki and I choose to hold space for the living and the dead who live on and bless us still. When John's family looked into his dark eyes, they said that they saw the depths between the worlds.

As Vicki continues to receive babies, she remembers her nephew and understands the connection between us and our ancestors. Once we experience infant death, we do not take life for granted. John Gilbert is an excellent midwife's assistant. He is there with Vicki, especially in those dark hours of the night that remind us of the ocean's mysteries, when women labor as they wait for the light of the sun and the warmth of their newborns' bodies in their arms.

Isaiah's Promise

FOR FIVE MONTHS OF MY SECOND PREGNANCY I knew that my unborn baby would die. Unable to sleep at night after a routine ultrasound revealed several anomalies, I went online. I typed "trisomy 18," "infant death," "genetic defects," "pregnancy without a baby," but none of my searches satisfied me. I'm not sure what I was looking for, perhaps a literary essay grappling with the reality of a pregnancy that would end in death. Perhaps I was looking for some discussion of shamanism to help me understand my place in my pregnancy.

After reading through the medical information about trisomy 18, I found some writings that were difficult for me. I read a book by a woman who could not believe that her baby died when she had asked Jesus for a miracle. There were a few blog posts and articles that said that if you have faith in God, then you demand your miracle and you fight the diagnosis. I was perplexed. I did not grow up in a Christian faith that makes demands on God, though perhaps we have all done this at some point. I understood the Orthodox Christian Faith to be the faith of Mary, the Mother of God, who said, "Be it unto me according to Thy word" (King James Bible, Luke 1:38). The faith of St. Seraphim of Sarov and St. Xenia, of St. Mary of

Egypt, fool for Christ, St. Anthimos of Chios and St. Nectarios, the humble bishop of Aegina. Again and again our saints and teachers tell us that we have to submit to the reality of our lives, to God's will, fate or karma. Whatever language we use, we are walking the path of life, and challenges appear out of nowhere. Our American culture does not offer much support for those of us going through life-threatening and grief-filled situations. I could not change Mary Rose's diagnosis, but I could honor her life and her death.

Several weeks after finding out about my unborn child's condition I came upon the book *For the Love of Angela* by Nancy Mayer-Whittington. I read it at night when I could not sleep. I was relieved to have found a book that resonated with my situation. Nancy, who is Catholic, had a few miscarriages between her eldest daughter and her pregnancy with Angela, who died of trisomy 18 shortly after birth. The book has short chapters, which were perfect for someone in my state of mind. Nancy writes of her acceptance of her daughter's condition, her path and grief, and her work to use her circumstances for some good. In one of the poignant moments in her book, she writes about hearing a song on the radio that had been played at her wedding and embracing her pregnant body to dance with her unborn child. Nancy knew that she would not have the chance to sway and dance with her child in her arms after birth, so she enjoyed this precious moment with Angela. I cried and finished the book quickly. Then I wrote an email to Nancy.

I read in the book that Nancy and Cubby LaHood, whose newborn also died, founded a nonprofit organization to support parents who choose to continue pregnancies after a fatal or life-threatening diagnosis. In my grief and shock it didn't occur to me that I could ask for help from Isaiah's Promise. I wrote to thank the writer for her book and to let her know how much she was comforting me. Within a few days I had an email from Cubby, who mentored me throughout the pregnancy and who remains a dear friend. Cubby asked for my address, and within two days I had beautiful gifts coming to my door. Isaiah's Promise sent presents for my unborn baby when most people would not consider such a thing. Their volunteers made a beautiful pink and white blanket with roses and Mary Rose's name. They sent the book *Letters to John Paul: A Mother Discovers God's Love in her Suffering Child* by Elena Kilner, a prayer shawl, and other thoughtful gifts that surrounded our few moments with Mary Rose. Cubby, whose infant son, Francis, died many years ago, has lived her life in service to others. I did not know that she had cancer as she wrote to me. She didn't want to add any more stress to my difficult pregnancy by sharing her own struggles.

Isaiah's Promise cites the scripture from Isaiah 49:15: "See, I will not forget you. I have carved you on the palm of my hand." They have a beautiful documentary on their website interviewing a few of their families, and they recently published an

Isaiah's Promise Tribute Book honoring a few of the babies in their 25-year history. I am honored that Mary Rose is featured in those holy pages among so many intercessors.

Isaiah's Promise does not hide from the reality of babies with genetic defects and their subsequent deaths. The organization teaches us to be compassionate even to those whom our society discards or ignores. We can all become more sensitive to those with illnesses and fragilities, not just our babies who are challenged from the womb, but our elderly and our bereaved. Nancy and Cubby met decades ago and decided that together they would support others going through the challenges of similar pregnancies. Instead of hiding from the presence of other children, who would no doubt remind them of their own deceased babies, they embraced dozens of children who were deformed, defected and perfectly beautiful. I count Nancy and Cubby as my life teachers. Instead of putting Mary Rose behind me, as some would want me to do, I am taking her with me on my path. I will pause along the way to offer love and comfort to other mothers whose babies die too soon. Loving our children unconditionally is easy when we have a community to uphold us in prayer, love and action.

It's Not Your Business: A Discussion of Abortion and Neonatal Life Support

I HEARD THE POET CLARIBEL ALEGRIA speak at *The Resilience of the Human Spirit Conference* in 2006. She said that everything we do is political. During my pregnancy with Mary Rose, I recalled her words often. Choosing to carry my daughter to term after testing revealed that she had trisomy 18 disturbed people, and my pregnant body became a part of public discourse. Not too many expectant mothers know that their baby will die, and though I am pro-choice politically, I am also a private person who still does not understand why people freely offered me advice on two decisions that most have no experience making: abortion and neonatal life support.

A few Christian friends suggested abortion, and this surprised me. Did it surprise me because they were talking and posting on Facebook about God, or was it because I thought that my decision to carry my baby was private? I would never tell my very closest friends what to do with a pregnancy. What made it okay for acquaintances to tell me what to do with my pregnancy?

It was appropriate for the doctors and genetic counselor to offer me the choice of abortion. When I said no, that was it, perhaps because I live in the south, and Christianity is the mainstream culture here. I know other mothers are pressured into aborting their babies and have a hard time finding doctors who will work with them to carry their pregnancies to term. I know that some parents of babies with trisomy 18 can't find doctors to treat their children because they are deemed incompatible with life. It seems that no matter what we do, there are challenges. I did a few things that were not expected: I carried my baby to term, birthed her at home, and did not have her body taken to a funeral home. I insisted on making my own way through a system that doesn't offer many choices.

I can't imagine that abortion is an easy decision. There is still a loss. When I was mourning after my baby died, postpartum hormones raging, I knew that some people thought I wouldn't be going through this if I had terminated my pregnancy. It's not so simple. I know women who have had abortions and they are still dealing with their choice years later, just as I will always walk my path with the consequences of my choice to birth and bury my newborn.

I was childless for 15 years, not by choice. In that decade and a half, I wanted to be pregnant. I wanted a child of my own with every cell of my body. I knew that I could not terminate a pregnancy regardless of the child's outcomes even when a child was an abstract wish far off in the future. I first felt Mary Rose move in the genetic counselor's office as she was asking me if I would have an abortion. I firmly stated *No*. I wished for a child, and I had a child.

My husband and I agreed that we would not terminate the pregnancy and then decided that we did not want life support for our newborn. If our baby could not breathe on her own, could not eat, or suck, we wanted to hold the space to honor her peaceful death. We were making these intense decisions with our neonatologist, midwife and priest, and then someone would say, *You didn't have an abortion*? I have one question: Why is this any of your business?

The decision to carry a child with a fatal illness to term or not, to choose life support for an unborn baby or not, to plan a funeral instead of readying a nursery, these are all private decisions. For those who feel that they should weigh in, let me stop you here. Only if a couple asks, *What should we do*? is it appropriate to give advice. In our case we never asked anyone for advice, except for our midwife, doctors and our priest. We wanted to be sure that our decisions were ethical, that we were not denying our daughter anything as her parents. But life is life. She would either breathe on her own, or she would not. She would either eat, or not. Mary Rose did neither.

For people who don't know what to say, say less. The comments I appreciated most were, *I don't understand what you are going through, but I'm here for you*. It is somewhat comical that people dispense advice easily with no experience in dealing with the current challenges. One mother told me, *I wouldn't do anything. Just wait and believe that God will heal your baby. Do you pray? Do you believe in miracles*? I believe in miracles, but I also believe in accepting God's will. I had carried a healthy child to term, and I knew that my daughter's body was not developing normally. If I had listened to this woman, what would we have done with Mary Rose's body?

She was buried within 26 hours of birth. I couldn't exactly wait to see what would play out when the tests are 99% accurate.

My friend Isabel's niece, Grace Miriam, has full trisomy 18, spina bifida and hydrocephalus. Most people would have aborted Grace, but her parents, who are devout Catholics, carried Grace to term. She is alive and breathes on her own. Grace has survived surgery on her spine and surgery to place a shunt in her brain. A priest told Grace's father that they should consider their time with Grace as Holy Hours.

We see life in the fragmentation of our individual lives, but what about the bigger picture of one, connected, pulsing Universe? How many lives is Grace touching? Why do humans think that one life is more valuable than another? I think back on my pregnancy with Mary Rose and remember feeling vulnerable and alone. If your friend or sister or cousin has had a troubling ultrasound or a miscarriage, consider offering her a box of tissues and a cup of tea. A hug. Shared tears. Unless you have ever been diagnosed with a pregnancy that is considered fatal, don't offer advice. You can't know what you would do until you are standing there, hands on your belly, at the crossroads, feeling your child move, loving her no matter what.

A Mother's Grief Reaches into the Belly of the Earth

I AM THINKING OF DEMETER AGAIN. I see an image of her roaming the earth searching for her daughter, Persephone. I am pregnant. My unborn daughter will die sometime after birth if I'm lucky enough to meet her alive. My pregnant body swells. My daughter moves for a few weeks and then I barely feel her.

I remember studying Greek mythology in school. I was in the seventh grade at St. Demetrios Greek Orthodox School in Astoria, New York, when we were assigned Edith Hamilton's book by Ms. Cathro, the teacher who taught me how to diagram sentences. I remember Persephone and Hades, the pomegranate, the red succulent seeds. Now as an adult with my hormones raging, I think of Demeter, the grieving mother.

I cannot nest. There will be no nursery. I change toilet seats instead and weep over the toilet bowls. *How is this my fate?* When strangers congratulate me, I stare at them blankly. And there in my mind is Demeter. She rages. She wears loose robes that flow around her form like a strong wind. I feel her keening in my body. Grief wells up inside of me and I sob. I know what it is like to lose a child, though I have not lost her yet. Demeter roams the earth looking for her daughter. Her grief stops the blooming of the earth. It is a force. I rage with her.

Only I have no place to run. I can barely walk from my grief and sciatic pain by the end of the pregnancy. I sit in pain. I limp. My form is crooked. My baby shudders inside me and I imagine that she is having seizures. People tell me to have faith, that she will be healed, that she could be born healthy. Everything I do for her is accompanied by weeping.

In Rachel Zucker's poetry book *Eating in the Underworld*, Persephone says, "the body of my mother is everywhere" (5). Persephone is looking to leave her mother by entering the underworld. Demeter is everywhere looking and searching but not finding her daughter. There is power in this grief, but there is also madness. I start to intuit more, to see more. My eyes see prisms of light before a terrible migraine. I see my ancestors surrounding me. Matina. Yiayia. Mother Mary. They tell me that I can do this. I can face my biggest fear, because my child will die.

I birth my daughter two weeks late, after 21 days of contractions. I hold her in my arms and look at her weak form and know that we don't have time. *Get my mother now*, I tell one midwife. *Bring my son.* The other midwife looks at Mary Rose and says, *Baby Girl, open your eyes and look at your mama.* Mary Rose, whose limbs are splayed from no muscle tone, opens her eyes and finds my face with her eyes. They are blue. I continue having contractions, and then soon after I birth the placenta, she slips away and I nestle my still baby wrapped in a blanket in my arms.

In *Women Who Run with the Wolves* Clarissa Pinkola Estés tells the story of Demeter and another Greek goddess, Baubo. Dr. Estés tells us, "she flew out over the land like a great bird, searching, calling for her daughter" (337).

We bury Mary Rose the next day. My milk comes in the day after that. *Your whole body is weeping*, says the midwife. *Mary Rose is a phantom limb.* I wake up at night looking for my baby. My body asks, *Where is my baby?* My body yearns for its offspring.

Dr. Estés writes, "Demeter raged, she wept, she screamed, she asked after, searched every land formation underneath, inside, and atop, begged mercy, begged death, but she could not find her heart-child" (337–338). After I bury my daughter I want to die. My heart feels shattered like bone. I am weighed down with heaviness. My grief reaches into the belly of the earth. I want the earth to take me into her so that I can be with my baby.

In speaking of Baubo, the goddess who appears to Demeter when she is completely spent from exhaustion and grief, who laughs and ignites Demeter's fire to continue her search, Dr. Estés says, "we only need one shard in order to reconstruct the whole" (337). I am shards of shattered heart. How do I reconstruct myself?

It is Autumn and the earth is changing. Demeter must say good-bye soon, and so she starts to withdraw her energy from the earth. Soon the plants and trees will be resting from their work. Soon winter will come and we will feel the naked truth: that life and death are irrevocably woven together, that to live on this planet we must let go again and again. We give our babies and our parents and our friends over to the spirit world, into the depths of the earth.

We weep like Demeter, but we won't have them back for a few months out of each year. We howl. We keen. But then we brush off the dust and walk on. We take our broken parts and carry them with our pain and walk on until we can transmute that pain. Spring does come again no matter how cold the winter might be.

Home Birth and a Fatal Diagnosis

Tell people: A woman's confidence and ability to give birth and to care for her baby are enhanced or diminished by every person who gives her care, and by the environments in which she gives birth.

Arielle Greenburg and Rachel Zucker

I HAVE TWO FRIENDS WHO SAY that they each know two babies who died at home because of a midwife. I'm not sure who these babies are and what the reality is. Babies sometimes die, though we like to pretend that this never happens. They die in hospitals and they die at home, though thankfully most of our babies live and thrive. I chose to birth my babies at home, and it still surprises me to watch people's responses. Home birth makes many people uncomfortable. I believe that every woman has the right to make her own decision about where to birth. If I would have been better served in a hospital, I would have birthed there, but I preferred to be in a quiet place with lots of time to let my body do what it had to do as the gateway and entryway for my children's lives on earth.

Initially I thought that I had to have a hospital birth for Mary Rose because of her trisomy 18 diagnosis. I lost my footing after that life-changing ultrasound. My midwife decided to leave her practice, and I was going to meet the midwife, Grace, who would take over. My two-year-old son wasn't sleeping through the night. He woke me at least two times each night and refused to nap. I was already in a fog of exhaustion when the ultrasound technician tensed up and left to get the doctor.

After a diagnosis like trisomy 18 there are several doctors' appointments. I went for an ultrasound of the heart because my daughter had a severe heart defect. The hospital wanted monthly ultrasounds, but we refused this monitoring. Not a week after our ultrasound we got a phone call from a peppy woman identifying herself with the hospital who was conducting a research study. She basically said, *I heard that your baby has trisomy 18. I would like her blood which we can extrapolate from your blood. You'll get a $25 Target gift card.* No thank you.

From there we visited a kind pediatric cardiologist, who gets the big picture of life. He did not recommend surgery for Mary Rose even if she was born alive. He would work with us to give her medicine to keep her comfortable, but he said that she probably would not live as long as three months in the best of circumstances.

The cardiologist cleared me for a home birth and wrote a letter saying as much. I visited again with the high-risk ob/gyn toward the end of the second trimester and was told that I was not at any additional risk due to Mary Rose's trisomy 18. Although the doctor prefers a hospital setting, she did not object to a home birth. We then visited a neonatologist who was kind, except for one thing. When he described the defects of trisomy 18, he said, *She'll probably look cute to you.* Babies with trisomy 18 are often described as elfin, since they are small and have deformed ears. I felt stunned in that moment and afraid of what my daughter would look like once again. The doctor's words reminded me how different my child would be from healthy, thriving newborns.

It was a whirlwind of information, not enough information, medical appointments, stress, and uncertainty. That range – from stillborn through a few months – made it difficult for me to prepare myself emotionally. I slowly got a few things ready. My sister sent me very few newborn clothes that my niece wore two years earlier. Isaiah's Promise sent handmade blankets and gifts. I had a baptismal gown ready, and how I hoped that Mary Rose would be baptized, not because of any sin she had but because I wanted to welcome her into our faith with the sacrament. I got the pump out and bought bags to freeze milk. I bought a preemie car seat in case we did end up at the hospital and Mary Rose was too small for my son's infant car seat. Every time I walked through Target I wept and tried not to look at the pink cloud of baby clothes. I bought a few undershirts and pink socks. I vowed to do right by my daughter in life and in death. That meant buying a cemetery plot and a coffin, and deciding if we would put her on life support. My husband and I agreed that we would not extend her life briefly with machines. It did not feel right for our family, though I know other families choose differently.

I thought that we would be fine for our home birth, but there was a lot of drama with a nurse manager at pediatric hospice who thought that I wanted to kill my daughter because I didn't want to put her on life support. She threatened my midwife, telling her that the police could charge her with manslaughter if Mary Rose died at home. She turned our pediatrician against us by discussing the legal ramifications of Mary Rose's dying at home. (After checking with the neonatologist and the pediatric cardiologist, they confirmed that Mary Rose's case was sealed tight with thorough records. There would be no legal issues given the trisomy 18 diagnosis.) The pediatrician was initially comfortable coming to the house for a visit to diagnose Mary Rose with trisomy 18, but then he would not come. This nurse manager even took the DNR hostage. The pediatrician was supposed to mail it to me at home, but she called him and made sure that he sent it to hospice instead. She would not release it until I promised to birth in a hospital. I needed a DNR, a doctor willing to come to the house if my baby died before we could get to a specialist, and a licensed midwife. I prayed and hoped that these three pieces would come together. In hindsight, neonatal hospice would have been more appropriate for our needs, since pediatric hospice does not understand neonatal illnesses well.

The tidal wave that hospice brought to my life after I already had things in place for a home birth speaks to the way our society operates. There is a system in place, and everyone is expected to follow it. A home birth is unusual for most, and so is an infant with a neonatal illness. Pediatric hospice is very helpful when children are on life support and are facing death. The nurse, who was uncomfortable with my case, was operating from a place of fear. She was afraid of home births. She thought that Mary Rose would suffer in her death, which is not the case with newborn babies with trisomy 18. Instead of educating herself on neonatal illness, she went to war with me and used every pawn she could by trying to instill fear in the midwife and the pediatrician. The pediatrician bought into the fear of lawsuits. Thankfully our midwife, Grace, saw through it.

The controversy with home birth is real, but I am not writing a pro-home-birth piece here. I am writing to say that if a woman has birthed at home and wants to do so again, it is still an option. I was not prepared to have my daughter subjected to tests at birth. The hospital wanted her cord blood. And when she died, she would have to go through the morgue. *What about religious Jews, Bahá'ís and Orthodox Christians?* I asked. What if your religion and belief is to take care of your own dead? No one knew anything about this. I wanted to prepare Mary Rose's body for burial myself. The priest had the casket. We had the plot. I wanted her body released to me. No embalming. No refrigerator. My baby would go from my arms into the church. The doctor answered, *No exceptions. This has never come up before. We don't know. We just don't know.*

I felt like I was asking permission to birth on the moon, to send my daughter's body to the stars in a rocket. My wishes were simple. In the event that we only had a few minutes or a few hours or even a few days, I wanted to hold my daughter quietly and give her a peaceful life. I was not judging the current system or telling others what to do. I wanted this simple thing for my daughter. I wanted my son to meet her and hold her. I wanted the peacefulness of home.

On my 42nd birthday my son got sick, my back was completely out, my mother was coming in three more days to help, and on this day I found out that I could not birth at home due to hospice's interference. It was early July. We had a birth plan, lived a few minutes from a hospital, planned a funeral, and were as ready for life or death as we would ever be. I agreed to the hospital birth so that the nurse would give me the signed DNR. Then I decided that there had to be another way.

We finally found a doctor who would come to the house to diagnose my baby or to pronounce her dead. A child cannot technically be diagnosed until she is born. We were all set, except that I was having contractions for three weeks but not progressing into active labor. I was stuck. How could I go through labor only to bury my baby? What if she was severely deformed? Would I love her? Yes! Yes! I wanted to nest but I couldn't. I got distracted when my family visited to meet Mary Rose. She waited. They went home. August came as the contractions kept steady.

After Mary Rose was born, I did some research and tried to find cases of home births for babies with trisomy 18. I only found one case in England. There were several women who started birthing at home, but they ended up in the hospital when they did not dilate. And for me, if I had another midwife who was less experienced or afraid, I would not have been able to birth at home. Grace gently used natural ways to encourage labor when my body stalled. Perhaps the placenta and baby with trisomy 18 do not give the body the proper signals. We have to consider the emotional response to a fatal diagnosis too. A woman in labor stands at the threshold of life and death. The soul is born and takes its first breath. It is a holy moment. I knew that Mary Rose would leave us. I hesitated. I did the best that I could.

I am grateful that I had several small miracles to allow me to birth my breech baby in a pool at home and hold her for the moments that were her life. She was barely breathing at birth, and after the placenta was birthed she slipped away. Mary Rose was born under the painting "Healing Companion," surrounded by a quiet and profound love. Her birth was a visitation that transformed those few people who were present. Mary Rose was born twice: once into our world and once into the next one where she is Light. She was not baptized, yet we were transfigured.

I am not telling my story because I want all women to give birth at home, and I respect the surgeons and hospital staff who help the babies who need them. However, for the mother who has known home births and who wants to birth a baby with trisomy 18 or 13 at home, please know that it can be done with a willing midwife who is knowledgeable and experienced. The medicalization of birth is another story. Our high infant mortality rates and high mother mortality rates in the hospital setting can be discussed at another time. If you are called to walk through a pregnancy with a fatal diagnosis, please make your own decision and allow for any possibility.

My midwife says that she wants people to stop being afraid of these babies. They live the lives that they are given, and in their defects they teach us to be true to ourselves and our path. I told my sister that my experience with Mary Rose felt like I was put into a centrifuge and, when everything stopped spinning, I wasn't the same person anymore. I couldn't see life in the same way anymore. Mary Rose focused me, broke me open to love more, to notice the yellow butterfly going by and the light coming through the pine tree. In our tiny fragment of time together there was profound truth and mercy. These babies are holy wherever they are birthed.

Stop This Mother's Milk!

THE NIGHT AFTER I BURIED my newborn daughter, my milk came in. I had hoped that I would be spared dealing with mother's milk. I was shocked and surprised that I was shocked. The pregnancy was over. Grief thick as molasses set in. I was physically sore after labor, and hormones woke me up at night looking for my baby to feed. I longed to hold my child, but she was a phantom limb. Hadn't I been through enough? Why milk, when Mary Rose was not here to drink it? It felt as if God were mocking me. My midwife, Grace, said that my whole body was weeping. I cried and cried, struggling to get around since my sciatic pain was still severe, wondering if I would survive being postpartum at all.

It was Sunday night, and my mother tried to bind my breasts while my husband slept and I cried from pain. The next morning the pain was excruciating. I wept and called my midwife who would come to help. My breasts looked like missiles about to launch. The pain was so intense that every movement hurt. Afterbirth pains continued. I remember sitting down a lot and weeping. After all that work, the months of pregnancy and labor, what did I have to show for my efforts?

When Grace came with essential oil of peppermint and a carrier oil, No More Milk tea and a bag from Rite Aid with Advil, ice packs and bandages, I felt her love in her blue eyes and ready hands telling me that I would be okay. I was writing a dark poem, moping in bed, frustrated that my back pain hadn't gone away immediately. She showed me how to massage the essential oil of peppermint in a carrier oil onto my breasts. I started to massage milk out for some relief. She spoke about the gift these babies are to those who encounter them unafraid, but I just wanted my milk to go away.

It took a few weeks for my milk to dry up completely. It took some time to piece together a how-to list to stop the milk. This is what worked for me:

1. Sudafed has been shown to dry up milk. I took a lot of Sudafed for about a week, and then took less for a second week.

2. Sage tea and No More Milk tea, both found in a health store or online at vitacost. com or luckyvitamins.com. I alternated the teas and drank them all day. I think that the sage tea worked better, but they both helped.

3. Cabbage leaves cold from the refrigerator did not seem to work. I read one study that said that cabbage leaves had not been shown to decrease milk sup-

ply, but acted as an ice pack and relieved some pain and pressure. I continued to look online until I found another source that said to activate the enzymes in the cabbage leaves, you had to crush the veins by going over each leaf with a rolling pin. I covered my breasts in crushed cabbage leaves and then placed ice packs on them. When the leaves wilted, I did it again. The crushed leaves did help.

4.   Essential oil of peppermint diluted in a carrier oil applied directly to breasts has been shown to slow milk supply. I did this two to three times a day.

5.   Hot baths to let the milk drip out. I sat in a bath and let my milk drip into the tub each night, sometimes massaging some milk out.

I did all of these things for at least two weeks and then started taking steps out. I stopped the Sudafed first, then the cabbage leaves, then the essential peppermint oil. I stuck with the teas for several weeks until my breasts no longer filled up with milk. I know that binding breasts has worked for women for centuries, but it was too painful.

After my first pregnancy I pumped milk for ten months for my son, until I became so ill that I had an autoimmune disorder. I did not get sick from pumping. It was a combination of not sleeping enough with a baby waking up every three or four hours, coxsackie virus, and the exhaustion of pumping day and night while taking care of a baby and a terminally ill aunt that put me over the edge.

Many mothers who carry children with fatal illnesses pump and donate their milk to a breast milk bank, helping others who have too little milk or no milk at all. After my experience with my son, I could not get back on the pump unless I had a child able to drink my milk. I felt selfish but I did not want another baby getting Mary Rose's milk. Perhaps this path of stopping my milk would have been easier if I had pumped and slowly weaned myself from pumping until the milk lessened, but I couldn't do it. In speaking to my bereavement doula, Leslie, she said that in her experience, mothers who are in shock and don't expect their babies to die often pump as part of their grieving process. She thought that I had been mourning Mary Rose during those long five months after her diagnosis and did not need to pump.

One week after my daughter's funeral I went to a pow wow with my doula, Leslie, and artist friend, Sindy. We sat on the grass under a tree listening to drumming, feeling the heartbeat of the earth moving forward, even when we want life to stop. The dancers came out in their colorful native clothes, moving and singing, celebrating their culture and way of life. A woman carrying a tiny newborn sat down in front of me. It was a big park. *Really?* I thought. My breasts ached, my body bled and I sat there trying not to cry, held up by the sisterhood of my companions. I didn't stay long because I was exhausted, but I walked around limping and bought a wooden frog for my son, knowing that the choice I would make was to continue on my path for as long as God kept me here.

It is my hope that each woman faced with milk after a miscarriage or infant death does what feels best. That first intuitive feeling in the heart center is right. Pump, if that feels right, and bless others with your milk. And if, like me, you just can't do it, don't. Either way, you will survive this time that feels endless and maddening. Those postpartum months were worse than I expected, especially because I couldn't sleep through the night. I would wake up after a couple of hours of sleep and toss and turn for hours. *Where is my baby?* I kept thinking. My eyes would dart around looking for the girl I wanted to hold and nourish.

Where is my baby? I like to think that she is right next to me, cheering me on. *You can do it,* she says to me. And so can you.

Trisomy 18: The Range of Possibilities

For Nora, who gives us hope.

ONE OF THE DIFFICULT THINGS about a trisomy 18 diagnosis is the range of possibilities. How can a mother prepare for her baby's birth when she might be born still or live for a few months? How do you prepare for labor? Is it time to get a nursery ready? How do you nest? I struggled a lot with this range during the pregnancy, and when Mary Rose died an hour after birth, I felt unprepared. That was it? Where were our tender, special moments? How could it be over so quickly after so much anticipation and such a long pregnancy? I know that I am one of the lucky ones. Though my daughter was barely breathing, I looked into her eyes and saw that they were blue.

When I wrote grants for a living, I depended on data to help me build my case for my projects. I am no stranger to research, and I know what to do with numbers when I get them. However, the numbers for trisomy 18 baffled me. The doctors give you a brochure that lists a number of defects that would frighten any pregnant woman. The brochure says that 92–95% of babies born with trisomy 18 die before their first birthday. The medical establishment says that trisomy 18 is incompatible with life. I wanted to know about the 5–8% who live.

Trisomy 18 is an illness with multiple defects. The child's brain is severely disabled. In the pictures that I have seen, the infant opens one eye, the jaw is slack, the fingers are in a different position, the chin is shorter, the feet are longer, the head is bigger, the ears are deformed. I read about these defects and worried that my child would be so deformed that I would have a negative reaction to her. I wondered how I would handle my daughter's illness if she lived. How would I manage my family's needs when I live far from my extended family? What would the impact be on my young son? I mentioned my fear to the genetic counselor toward the end of my pregnancy and told her that I was concerned that Mary Rose would live and suffer. I mentioned mosaicism, a condition that does not affect all the DNA and is a milder illness, and she blurted out: *Your baby has the full-trisomy 18.* I had agonized for months over this, but was never given the information that was apparent from the genetic testing.

I looked and looked for stories, for answers. Who lived? Why? I found a blog about a boy on life support who was three. I found a few other cases of children who were alive and young. Except for very rare exceptions, they were on life support and had undergone multiple surgeries and hospitalizations to deal with their organ defects. They breathed through a trach and were fed through machines. The exceptions seemed to be children with a mosaic form of trisomy 18. They are higher functioning, and often breathe and eat on their own.

According to my online searches, most of the 5–8% of babies with trisomy 18 who live appear to be on life support. The data seem skewed. For parents who choose not to use life support, what are the numbers? For parents who choose life support, what are the numbers? I asked doctors what would happen after my daughter's birth and was told repeatedly, *We don't know. We have to wait and see how strong she is when she is born.*

However, in the publication *Care of the Infant and Child with Trisomy 18 or Trisomy 13: A Care Book for Families*, I read that "5–8% of these infants live past their first birthday without extraordinary measures. And, once a child's age is greater than a year there is a 60% chance to live beyond age 5 years" (11). It is estimated that there are 200 people in the United States alive and older than one year old with trisomy 18 or 13.

It is important to note the controversy surrounding the term "incompatible with life." People are trying to remove this term from the description of trisomy 18. I know that very few babies with trisomy 18 or 13 live. The children who do live need doctors who will treat them (often doctors don't want to treat babies considered to be incompatible with life), but most do not have the programming in their bodies to thrive. In addition to the defects and the developmental disabilities, the children have incredibly weak muscle tone. This is why Mary Rose's jaw was slack, why her limbs were splayed in all directions when I held her in my arms. This is the reason that most of these babies cannot eat or eat enough. Their sucking motion is weak, if they can suck at all. As a mother of a daughter with trisomy 18 who died, the illness seems incompatible with life, and even though some live, most of these babies die. This is not to say that babies who live don't deserve to be treated by doctors in the most ethical way. I spoke to a neonatal cardiologist to see about heart surgery for Mary Rose, and he did not recommend surgery. He said that if she could live long-term after the surgery, he would operate, but the heart, he said, is one defect of many. He also informed us that most of the babies who undergo heart surgery in Mary Rose's condition never come off the trach. Was he being unethical? We never got to the point where surgery was an option, but my husband and I decided that we probably would not opt for it. We didn't want to cause any suffering for our unborn daughter.

This week I was very touched by the comments and emails and replies I got to my essay "Home Birth and a Fatal Diagnosis" that I posted on my blog. One woman reached out to me to tell me of her home birth in 2000. Her daughter, Nora, was born at home with full trisomy 18, and this is rare. I made the assumption that Nora was gone, like all the other babies I know with this illness. Nora's mother shared her story with me. Her daughter lives at age 15 without life support. I found some photos of her family on Facebook. Nora looks like an angel. Her eyes exude the deepest peace. I am so blessed to know her, to add her story to this work. Nora's story is rare. So how do we prepare for the different outcomes?

This week a baby with trisomy 18 was born under four pounds, and she lives. Grace Miriam had three diagnoses and lived for six weeks. Mary Rose slipped away peacefully after birth. Others are born still. How are we to know what will happen? When dealing with trisomy 18, as with all other things in life, we can only stay in the moment and breathe. As we all know, some moments change our lives forever. The accident, the diagnosis, the illness happens in one moment, and nothing is the same. This happens when we give birth. It happens when we hear news we don't want to know on an ultrasound. And it happens with trisomy 18. But our lives also change suddenly when we meet someone who lights up our soul, are offered a new job, hold a positive pregnancy test in our hand, and sometimes even when we witness a sunset dotted with birds migrating south for the winter. I am open to this continuously changing Universe, and I lift up my heart and pray one more time that whatever comes today is for the highest good of all.

Healing Companion

IT IS ALMOST A YEAR SINCE I MET the artist Sindy Strosahl. She came to my house on a rainy Wednesday to deliver my painting, "Healing Companion." I knew of Sindy through my midwife, who had one of her paintings of a pregnant woman in her office. I fell in love with the vibrant colors and decided that I would like to have an image to commemorate my two pregnancies, especially since I was childless for 15 years in what feels like another lifetime.

When we received news of our daughter's fatal condition, I messaged Sindy and told her. She meditated and connected to the soul of our unborn child and

"Healing Companion," © Sindy L. Strosahl

painted the image that you see here. When Sindy went to her car to get the painting, the torrential downpour stopped long enough for her to walk into my house. "Healing Companion" is a mixed-media collage. Sindy cut out pieces of the pages of a gardening book. I was excited when I saw words in Mary Rose's and my hair. My dress is fabric that she painted. The 3-D view of this image, with the ancestors as yellow orbs surrounding me, is so powerful that almost everyone who sees the original painting walks away with tears in their eyes.

Sindy, who also photographed Mary Rose's birth and witnessed her brief life, is now a doula. *Mary Rose changed my life*, she says. "Healing Companion" has comforted mothers around the world. I like to think of a web connecting the mothers who gaze at this image remembering their children. Some women do not birth living children. Some women do not have any living children. For many, these challenging pregnancies are their first.

It has taken me some time to acknowledge that the pregnant woman in "Healing Companion" is strong and graceful, that perhaps I am strong and graceful as Sindy painted me. In the painting, I am perfectly centered and focused on my pregnancy and baby. I neither felt strong during my pregnancy nor did I feel graceful as I limped around in extreme back pain for the last weeks waiting for my baby girl, still or breathing. But sometimes I catch a glimpse of my resolve in the image, and sometimes I feel that perfect peace knowing that everything is as it should be.

At the end of our lives, what will we remember? Who will greet us at the threshold between this life and the next? Certainly our children will usher us toward The Holy Light, and until then "Healing Companion" offers us a visual of how close our miscarried babies and our babies on the other side of the veil are. If you stand very still, you might hear a whisper of love or feel the brush of a tender touch.

The Bereavement Doula

DURING ONE OF MY PRENATAL VISITS, I mentioned that I wasn't sure if I should hire a doula for my second birth. I had been going to a number of doctors' appointments and did not have much time to think about my needs or labor. There was so much to do to confirm Mary Rose's diagnosis of trisomy 18, to plan for her birth and her death, to see specialists about her defects and to understand her illness the best that I could when medical doctors answered, *We don't know*, to my many questions. Midwife Gloria said, *You should hire a bereavement doula*. She suggested that I call Leslie Cuffee, and set up an appointment. Leslie was known in her community as a doula who could witness the death of a baby. Leslie's first birth as a doula was stillborn. When parents need her to walk them through a difficult pregnancy, she is present.

Expectant mothers hire doulas to support them through their labor and after the birth. A doula often spends more time with the mother during labor than a doctor or midwife. Doulas preserve the birthing space and do their best to work with providers to stick to the birth plan. They also seem to be experts at back massage just when the contractions crescendo. They know how to help a laboring woman through the hours of birthing.

When I met Leslie, she told me that I would write a book about Mary Rose. I looked at her, confused in my daze of shock and grief. *Forget your poetry and your novel. This is the book that will come first*, she said. Leslie felt that there was a need for a book about life and death and pregnancy, a book that embraced all babies regardless of their expected outcomes. Leslie told me of a birth where a baby was born with its organs outside of its body. She held the tiny body and told me that she was beautiful. I knew that Leslie would love Mary Rose in life and in death. She is one of the few who held my daughter after she died and smiled, looking at her face. She accepted God's will for Mary Rose and didn't question my daughter's value as a human being.

In her book *Birth, Breath & Death: Meditations on Motherhood, Chaplaincy and Life as a Doula*, Amy Wright Glenn discusses her spiritual path and her work as a doula and, later, as a chaplain. Many birth workers, be they midwives or doulas, turn to chaplaincy work. A doula holds the space for that newborn to be breathed. A chaplain holds the space for the last breath when the soul leaves behind the sacred vessel of this life and journeys on. It is holy work to witness the first and last breath. Glenn writes, "Learning how to live involves learning how to die. Love alone is the most potent power illuminating the breath's journey in between these thresholds. Love is the key. Love is the dance" (47). Mary Rose has taught me to embrace death fully as a part of life. How could I honor her without honoring her death? How could I love her and hold her without freeing her to do her sacred work?

Before I became pregnant with Mary Rose, I watched my aunt suffer and die from atypical meningioma. She was bedridden for nearly 18 months, her body betraying her desires to move and travel, yet she held onto this life. My pregnancy put my aunt's "young" death at age 64 into perspective, but I sometimes reflect on how gentle and peaceful Mary Rose's passing was, as opposed to my aunt's struggle and challenge to let go.

We are all going to die, though this seems to be what we fight most in our culture. Some of this is biological. The body will fight with all of its will and programming to survive, but there comes a point when we as a culture can begin to accept life's cycles. It is not good to live and bad to die. Death comes to all sentient beings, and we are transformed. Whether people believe in an afterlife or reincarnation or nothing at all past the breathing of this body, our bodies will be vacated and they will go back into the earth in some form and become something else: the flower, the field, the air we breathe.

Mary Rose's birth was long, but Leslie, my midwives and Sindy did not complain. They slept very little and walked with me as I gathered the courage I needed to let my baby go. In my body, Mary Rose was safe, but once born would she breathe? Would she eat? The hours before Mary Rose was born were holy. We laughed, practiced yoga, breathed and cried. And when the moment came to enter this world and this life, my daughter was welcomed and embraced.

Bereavement and birth work might seem contradictory, but sometimes life on earth is short. I am grateful that there are people who are brave enough to face life and death in the quiet and stillness that seems lost in most of our fast-paced, post-9/11 world. In her poem "The Summer Day," Mary Oliver asks, "what is it you plan to do / with your one wild and precious life?" I plan to be present for the transitions that await me and my loved ones. Like the doula, let's be present for our babies, our parents, our loved ones and even ourselves. Let us bless the bereavement doulas and the chaplains and the ministers who aren't afraid to hold our hands and wait with us as life breathes us, for the appointed hours.

The Holy Homeopath

I FIND MYSELF SURROUNDED by amazing women healers; they hold me up against the frailties of this world. When I was pregnant with Mary Rose, my tribe of healers included my therapist, doula, midwives, artist friends, massage therapist and homeopath. Yes, I use homeopathic remedies even though some believe homeopathy to be a placebo. I see homeopathy as holy healing, and I call Aniela Costello, my dear classical homeopath, The Holy Homeopath. The spiritual are one with the physical in this treatment, and Aniela sees me for who I am: a broken seeker who walks her path one step at a time, one breath, then another.

I'm not sure why homeopathy is a topic of controversy, but I recognize when people roll their eyes at me when I mention that homeopathic remedies have helped me. They work for millions of people in India, the Royal Family of England, and people all over Europe and the United States. In *Copeland's Cure: Homeopathy and the War Between Conventional and Alternative Medicine*, writer Natalie Robins offers documented research on how homeopathy was once taught at most medical schools in the United States until the American Medical Association (AMA) went to war and successfully took homeopaths out of their association. Why? Money. Homeopathic remedies are cheap and they work. Therefore, patients require fewer allopathic medicines. Where it was once considered unethical to advertise for any pharmaceutical, now the pharmaceutical industry is a powerful force in American health-care. To understand the extent that homeopathy was used by medical doctors in the 1800s and early 1900s, according to Robins, "More than 1,900 homeopathic doctors were commissioned in the army and navy during the [first world] war" (143).

I started homeopathic treatment in my late 20s. I have a primary care doctor and go when I need to, but I usually start with natural remedies, as they are easier on the body and have fewer side effects. Mary Rose was diagnosed by high-risk ob/gyns, and I continued to work within the medical system, seeing a neonatologist, infant cardiologist and other doctors. I could tell you the remedies that heal burns, fevers, poison ivy and an autoimmune disorder, but I want to talk about grief. There were at least two times during my pregnancy with Mary Rose when I cried until my body convulsed for so long that I thought I would never stop. The first time that this happened I texted Aniela. *I can't stop crying*, I wrote. *Ignatia*, was her reply. And within minutes my crying slowed and I was able to make dinner for my son. Even though my daughter had a fatal diagnosis, I ate well, took vitamins and supplements and refused to take any medicine, even for an excruciating nine-day headache. I love both of my children equally and did not want to treat my daughter with less respect and concern, even though she was expected to die. Under the care of my homeopath, I used ignatia from the shock of the diagnosis to the end of the pregnancy and the intense grieving period that followed Mary Rose's birth and death.

There is a heaviness in my heart center, I typed a few weeks later; *I can't bear the heaviness of this grief*. Aniela replied, *Take two doses of ignatia in one hour*. The ignatia sometimes held for five weeks or a couple of months, but once I cried uncontrollably or could not bear the heaviness of trisomy 18 and my grief, I would take a dose. The grief lifted a bit and I felt lighter in my heart. I met Aniela through an occupational therapist who is of the Bahá'i Faith. *She is the best*, Leigh said, *Go see her*. And for once someone used that phrase correctly. I drove to New York City with my fussy baby alone to meet this woman. She has been treating us both ever since. Aniela is also of the Bahá'i Faith. She often shares beautiful prayers with me, feeding my soul as she treats my body.

On August 8, Aniela left me a voice mail message after I texted her that Mary Rose was born and died. *We're all praying for you. We love you. We love you. We love you and we're praying for you and dear Mary Rose*. She rocked me in her lull of we-love-yous. A few days later there was a package with a Bahá'i prayer that is framed and hanging next to a picture of Mary Rose in my dining room. It says,

The Great Being saith:

The Tongue of Wisdom proclaimeth:
He that hath Me not is bereft of all things.
Turn ye away from all that is on earth and seek none else but Me.
I am the Sun of Wisdom and the Ocean of Knowledge.
I cheer the faint and revive the dead.
I am the guiding Light that illumineth the way.
I am the royal Falcon on the arm of the Almighty.
I unfold the drooping wings of every broken bird and start it on its flight.

Tablets of Bahá'u'lláh

I received it on Saturday, a week after Mary Rose's funeral, when I got home from a pow wow. I had just seen a falcon at one of the booths.

I think of homeopathy as prayer, a subtle energy of God, present in His/Her creations (because God is bigger than either gender), lifting us gently out of imbalance and restoring our life force and energy. It is a long journey, and though we are moving on from ignatia to balance me from my difficult pregnancy, I will always be grateful for the remedy, so subtle it could help a weeping mother wipe away her tears and reach for a knife to cut tomatoes for her son's dinner.

I call Aniela holy. To be holy is to be fully human and to embrace life, which also includes death. It is to breathe in communion with every other sentient being and know that we are all connected. Only by walking in unity with each other and Creator and Earth can we build the communities that will embrace and support life in all its forms, with healthy DNA or trisomies, with love, always with love.

The Midwives

AN ANONYMOUS MEDICAL COMPLAINT was made against one of my midwives, and I cannot use their names in this book. The week of Mary Rose's one-year anniversary of her birth and death, I had a message from Elizabeth asking questions about the birth. I asked her what was going on, and she told me that she believed that one of her friends and confidantes had sent my Facebook post thanking her for being at Mary Rose's birth to the Medical Board, alleging that I did not have adequate prenatal care. My baby died, and someone used my dead baby to hurt Mary Rose's midwife. I was stunned and angry. I cannot honor two of the important people who allowed me to have my home birth by using their names. So I changed their names to Grace and Elizabeth.

Grace and Elizabeth took over the practice of my first midwife mid-pregnancy. Elizabeth has a Virginia license, and Grace did not. Grace was not calling herself a midwife but instead called herself a birth consultant. She had attended half a dozen trisomy 18 and 13 births in her career of delivering over 3,000 babies. She took care of me and my baby with tenderness and deep understanding of the value of my daughter's life. Grace would look at me and say, *These babies are sweet. These babies are beautiful. These babies are angel babies.* . . . She wanted Mary Rose to live for a little while. She wanted me to have time with my daughter. She brought gifts for Mary Rose. Tiny pants and socks. A stuffed baby in a peapod. She made a pencil drawing of a baby's head coming out of a rose.

There were four or five weeks when Mary Rose did not grow at all. I knew that week 36 was approaching. Grace had told me that if I made it to week 36, Mary Rose would probably be born alive. Even though many of these babies are delivered early (sometimes by the choice of the obstetrician), there are also babies with trisomy 18 who are considered late, over 42 weeks, that grow at the end and are born alive. This was the case with my daughter. She had a growth spurt those last few weeks and was born alive at six pounds three ounces. And Grace was right, Mary Rose was beautiful even with her defects.

Grace now has her license restored after a legal situation that has taken years to resolve. This is the norm for midwives. It seems that there are folks ready to complain and do anything in their power to keep midwives from doing their work at home. I am not advocating for all women to birth at home. Many women do need hospital interventions, but women like myself who want to be home and who are not high-risk (except by the definition of being over age 35, which is ageist) have the right to birth at home. Let's understand this to be an issue of money. Hospitals charge tens of thousands of dollars, and insurance companies pay that easily, but our health insurance, Tricare, would not pay $3,500 for my home birth. It is illegal to birth at home in some states, such as Illinois. Many midwives have their licenses taken away or are jailed. Some midwives cannot work in their field any longer. Some of the stories sound like the witch hunts of Salem, Massachusetts.

Elizabeth and Grace attended births together. Grace drove two hours each way to take care of me. Elizabeth had access to my records and was well informed about my pregnancy. Because I was going through so much, with hospice and sciatic pain and planning the funeral, Elizabeth and I did not meet before the birth. I knew that Elizabeth had a brother who died of trisomy 18 and that she was a competent midwife. I trusted Grace who was my birth consultant to keep Elizabeth apprised of my health and pregnancy. My labor went beautifully despite Mary Rose's outcomes.

That Facebook post that sits on someone's desk at the medical board in an anonymous complaint dated August 9, 2014, says,

Thank you to the amazing circle of women who walked with me through this most difficult pregnancy and labor to birth my Mary Rose. I had contractions on and off for 21 days and labored longer than I did for my son. I knew that once I saw Mary Rose we would know how sick she was, and it was so. She did not have the mechanics or strength to breathe on her own. Thank you, my goddesses, earth mothers who bravely witnessed Life and Death with me not just yesterday, but for the past five months. Grace, Sindy, Leslie you are forever in my heart. Grace, I don't think I will ever meet a midwife so willing to walk through mire and muck to pave the way to birth at home for a fatally ill baby. What an uphill battle for that little girl! And how grateful I am to have had that one hour in our home loving Mary Rose. Thank you Elizabeth for stepping in yesterday with gentle kindness, meeting me for the first time in my grief. . . . I am so very blessed and humbled to have you in my life.

My Facebook photo is the photo of Sindy's painting "Healing Companion." The screenshot of this post, written in the rawness and shock of grief, was used by someone trying to take Elizabeth's license away without the courage to sign her name to the complaint. Whatever the motives are (I wonder if they are financial, since Elizabeth's practice is growing), filing a complaint without my knowledge or permission has defiled the memory of my baby. I don't understand how a party unfamiliar with a birth or the mother can make a medical complaint that is being taken seriously.

Grace's license has been restored; Elizabeth stands to lose her license. Elizabeth had to reopen the files of Mary Rose's birth and submit paperwork. She will be interviewed, and, if the board does not dismiss this claim, she will have to go before a committee for a hearing.

Mary Rose, my daughter who died of trisomy 18 at home because of the kindness and bravery of Grace and Elizabeth, pray that this complaint may be dropped and that your midwives can continue their blessed work on this earth.

The Cemetery

FOR THOSE WHO WISH TO BURY their babies in a cemetery, check with the cemetery after purchasing the plot to see what type of casket is needed. We didn't do this, and, after that long labor, while I carried my still baby in my arms, our priest, Father John, Tim and Grace were on the phone because we had a glitch in our funeral plans. Only vaults could be buried at the cemetery where we bought a plot. I had ordered a coffin from an Orthodox couple in South Carolina. The box was hand carved with an Orthodox cross, but it was not a vault. Father John had been kind enough to accept delivery of the coffin so that we didn't have it in our house in the room that would have been the nursery.

We did not wish to go through a funeral home and give our baby over to refrigeration or embalming. Since we had our home birth, we were able to prepare Mary Rose's body and hand her over to our priest to take her into the church, where parishioners would read psalms over her body until her funeral the next day. Our dear friend, Annie Consolvo, put us in touch with a funeral director whom she knew, and Joe was able to help us with paperwork for the death certificate (which we received in the mail before her birth certificate) and procure the appropriate vault/coffin for the burial. It was ugly. It was gray and looked like plastic, nothing I would have chosen, but after all my work to have my home birth, there wasn't an ounce of advocacy left in me. My daughter was dead. I had labored after carrying her full-term, and now I would face the dreaded postpartum period without her.

Grace, Father John and Tim tried hard to step around the system, but we acquiesced. Grace and I prepared Mary Rose's body. We washed her gently with a cloth and rubbed Weleda baby lotion on her body. We put a flower in her hair, turned her on her side and took pictures. We put the diaper that Sindy sewed with flowers on her, then a tiny undershirt. My mother and I dressed Mary Rose in her baptismal gown: silk with pink roses. I couldn't bear to cover her head with the hat, and I kept it. Around her neck we clasped a tiny gold cross from my sister who would have been her godmother or *νονά*. Kisses.

I lay Mary Rose in the box in disbelief. *I can't believe I'm doing this.* I close the box. I watch Father John carry her tenderly down the stairs and out the front door.

Birth Announcements after a Newborn Death

WHEN YOU ARE PREGNANT WITH A CHILD who might die before birth, is it appropriate to send birth announcements? For families who sent birth announcements for their older children, or for families who want to share the joy of their child, even though the child might not live long or be born still, it is important to follow your heart. It is appropriate to send out birth announcements for a stillborn baby or newborn who has died, if that is a parent's desire. Dr. Jessica Zucker has created infant loss birth announcements in her therapeutic work supporting grieving mothers. (See Resources.) Parents have choices in how to announce the birth of a baby, even when the baby's life ends before or soon after birth.

Mary Rose is my second child. I had joyously sent out birth announcements for my son two years earlier. I wanted to do the same for my beloved daughter. There was the problem of the relatives who did not acknowledge Mary Rose. There were many who could not handle my pregnancy – people who told me that an abortion would have been better than carrying to term. I did not want these people to see my daughter's photo. I only wanted people who loved her, people who opened their heart to her, to bear witness to her life and her physical form.

There is a nonprofit organization called Now I Lay Me Down to Sleep that sends volunteer professional photographers to photograph a birth with potentially fatal outcomes. They do a photo shoot when the baby has died and create beautiful memories for the families that have too little time. I had mixed feelings about this. Did I want photos of my baby when she was dead? Did I want to put flowers in her hair or pose her after she had passed away? The answer is yes. I never liked photos of people in their coffins, but since the only dress Mary Rose ever wore was for her burial I did ask my friend Sindy to take a photo of her in church.

After Mary Rose was born I sent out an email to many people. Following is an excerpt:

Hello Friends,

I am writing to announce the birth of our beautiful daughter, Mary Rose. She was born on Friday, August 8, and was with us for about an hour. Mary Rose surprised us in many ways, such as her breech birth and her size at 6 lbs. 3 oz. I birthed her at home, and she lived a life of love and peace. Mary Rose did not have the capacity or strength to breathe on her own. She died peacefully in my arms soon after birth, and was buried yesterday afternoon. During the funeral service Fr. John reminded us that love does not die with the body but continues into eternity. . . .

May Mary Rose's memory be eternal.

Love, *Dianna*

I posted a few photos of the birth on Facebook, and people did not know how to respond. What do you say? How do you respond to the photo of the newborn who has died? Many people did nothing, said nothing, sent nothing. The way that I reconciled my desire to send out a birth announcement while recognizing the disparity of warm, kind people showering us with support and the others who could not deal with Mary Rose was to create a thank you card with Mary Rose's photo. I decided that only the people who had reached out to us would get her birth announcement. I would honor my daughter by honoring the people who loved her and were kind to us. In sending out memorial thank you cards to those who expressed sympathy to us, I was able to create a different version of a birth announcement and honor her and our family as a whole.

I chose a pink thank you card online that held three photos. The photo on the front is the photo on the dedication page of this book. I have a passage by Edgar Cayce underneath that says, "For, each soul enters with a mission. We all have a mission to perform." I had chosen a scroll with this passage on a visit I made to Cayce's center in Virginia Beach during my pregnancy. Inside the card I put a family photo. My husband is wearing a Popeye t-shirt. My face is bent over my son's smiling face as I give him a kiss, and in my arms, my fingers tightly clutching her, is my daughter, my Mary Rose, wrapped in her blanket from Isaiah's Promise. Is she living? Is she dead? I do not know. She slipped away so quietly that I do not know the minute that she left her broken body. There is one more excerpt of a prayer under our family photo. I thank people for their expressions of sympathy, and on the back there is a small photo of my darling girl. She is naked and turned on her side, her beautiful features present, her arm curled under her face. Underneath is her only date: August 8, 2014.

When people reach out to me I sometimes send a photo of Mary Rose. I want people to know that she is part of our family, a beloved child, very much a part of the Vagianos and Armentrout families. If you want to honor your baby by making a birth announcement, then please do so. It is appropriate. It is a good way to honor her life. It is an acknowledgement of your pregnancy. We do not hold our babies for long, but there is no reason why we should not display our babies' photos and share them with this world that could benefit from intercessors who lived fully in a short time. The soul is perfect and complete even when the body is too broken for life on earth.

I know of families whose babies were deformed, whose children were born still, who did not want to share photos of their babies with others. Sometimes a photo of a foot or a hand is enough. Sometimes just the birth date with a small graphic of a teddy bear will do. There are many ways to honor our children and ourselves as mothers and fathers and grandparents. I only want to give you permission to do what feels right. Sometimes doing nothing feels right. Sometimes creating a card feels right. Whatever your baby looks like, she is your child and a part of your family forever.

The Memory Box

MAKE A PRETTY BOX, Cubby writes in her email, *or buy one. Put Mary Rose's things in there to remember her.* I find a wooden box at Michael's, as well as stickers welcoming a baby girl. I pause. My baby is dead, I don't get stickers and a double stroller, but then I remember how much we wanted her and welcomed her, waited for her and longed for her. I buy the box, decorative flowers and butterflies, and the stickers. *BABY GIRL. She's finally here. Bundle of Joy.*

The sympathy cards continue to bring up emotions. I spread them out, save a few and cut out images from the rest to decorate the box. I paint the box white and begin to glue fabric flowers and butterflies, then add words from the cards. *I will never be the same, reassurance, everlasting love.* I cut Mary Rose's name out of handwritten cards that two friends had sent. I work into the early morning hours because I am ready to take Mary Rose's few possessions out from my dresser drawer. I had clutched each item, weeping, during my nesting period, wondering if my baby would live long enough to wear anything at all.

My birth team painted preemie undershirts when they gave me a blessingway. A blessingway is an occasion that showers the expectant mother with blessings, instead of the more common baby shower that focuses on the baby. The term comes from the Navajo tradition and is also known as a Mother Blessing. One of Grace's friends, Jill Diana, who never met me, painted a onesie with Mary Rose's name on it. *She has an angel baby too,* Grace had said as she handed me gifts from an unmet sister. A dear friend and artist, Lakshmi, whose son, Siddha, died of trisomy 18, painted a onesie for Mary Rose with a pink flower. She started making these beautiful clothes to honor her son. Sindy sewed two diapers for Mary Rose. We buried our daughter in one, and I kept the other. I also kept the hat that came with her baptismal gown. I wanted something to hold onto. It has the beautiful roses that decorated her burial gown. Sindy also gave us a flower for her hair. When Grace and I were preparing Mary Rose's body for burial, we put it on and took a few pictures.

I place a few sympathy cards on the bottom of the box, and then add some comforting pink construction paper hearts that my first doula, Raizy, cut out and sent me with holy words she wrote in permanent marker: courage, *LOVE, surrender.* Next, Mary Rose's few never-worn clothes, followed by her blankets from Isaiah's Promise, my flower crown from the blessingway, and the baby pea in the pod that Grace brought before I labored. The empty box that once held the tiny cross from my sister, the flower barrette, my pink bracelet from the blessingway, and the scroll from Edgar Cayce's Center that I chose from a bowl when I was pregnant: *For, every soul enters with a mission. We all have a mission to perform.*

The box still needs something. My last step is to make color copies of cards that I had pulled from the *Mother Mary Oracle* deck by Alana Fairchild and Shiloh Sophia during my pregnancy. I glue them to the inside top of the box. Number 11, *Our Lady of Manifest Miracles.* Number 12, *Our Lady of Peaceful Change.* Number 29, *Our Lady of Starting Over.*

The box sits on the floor of my bedroom not far from "Healing Companion." I don't know if making a box will help other mothers, but, even in mourning our miscarried babies, we can name them and honor their presence in our lives. Perhaps there is a blanket or rattle that you purchased for the exciting day that you would meet your child. The blanket still means something, even if the child has moved on from this life quickly.

In her book *Naming the Child: Hope-filled Reflections on Miscarriage, Stillbirth, and Infant Death*, Jenny Schroedel writes, "While the world we live in views tears as a sign of weakness and so often strives to avoid them . . . tears have long been associated with intimacy with God, with wholeness, with a courageous and life-giving openness to the spiritual world" (82). Those who mourn are tearful. We express our emotions and honor our loved ones on the other side, as well as our own path of motherhood and grief. This ground is holy and healing. To move forward I will stay on this floor a little longer, longing for the baby who was once in my arms, touching her few things, remembering the life that was, the Life that is. . . .

The Truth about Positive Thinking

I READ A BOOK BY A FAMOUS NEW AGE writer after I found out about Mary Rose's trisomy 18 diagnosis, and I was taken aback when she said that she believed that all illness stems from negative thought. This includes any cold a child might get or a cancer. According to the writer, someone in the house has a negative thought and it takes hold in a child's body, causing sickness. I do believe that we attract much through our energy and thought patterns, but Mary Rose's trisomy 18 was a genetic illness, and I neither attracted nor created it. It troubles me that we blame each other for our children's illnesses (and our own), whether through negative thoughts or lack of faith.

Years ago, I was married to a man who was mentally ill and unable to keep a job. I reached a low point when my friends and family were having babies and going on vacation, while I could not afford groceries or gas for my car. My idea of the good life was being able to afford children and vacation. I read Elizabeth Harper's book *Wishing: How to Fulfill Your Heart's Desires* in the winter of 2009 and decided that I wanted a different life. I prayed and wished for a nurturing and loving partner (I called him my Wish Husband), children, a safe and peaceful home and abundance. I tucked my wishes away on my altar that sat on a piece of turquoise velvet fabric on the floor of my unfurnished bedroom and waited. I started practicing Qigong. I studied with Pat Bolger and took a Level 1 training for Emei Qigong. I meditated and prayed, and worked on my thought process. I was tired of coming home to the telephone or electricity being shut off, or tax notices on my door.

It took another 18 months, but I found the courage to walk away from the marriage after nearly 19 years with this broken man whom I had met when I was 18. I discovered many debts in my name after I left. But the wishes and prayers worked. I found an amazing lawyer, Debra Marino, dedicated to helping her clients. She fought for the condo to cover the debts that were left in my name. I went to visit my sister and her family in Switzerland. When I came back, I signed the divorce papers, and I went to the wedding of a friend dressed in orange and purple and gold. I was free from debt and the burden of an unhappy marriage and decided that I was okay being single and childless. I walked into St. Paul's Cathedral in Hempstead, New York, and there was one other person in the church. I am married to him now, and we have two children. Wishes do come true. But I cannot believe that all of our suffering comes from negative thoughts. My positive thinking may have been a catalyst in shifting my grim situation, but there has still been tragedy since then.

I've been thinking a lot about positive thinking since I carried Mary Rose. I remember being on the table of a naturopathic physician in New Haven many years ago. She blamed my negative thoughts for my pain and state of health. I remember feeling so small on her table, as I did when I was a child and my mother or teacher criticized me. I have studied various spiritual traditions in an effort to better myself for years, but lately I've been thinking that I don't have to get better. I can accept that I live in a fallen world and that sometimes the people I love get sick. I once had a student in my office telling me about her mother who had lost her battle with cancer. I looked her in the eyes and told her, *Your mother got sick and died. She is not a loser. She completed her life on earth.* Why do we beat each other down with our words, blaming thoughts for cancer or the flu or any other illness?

The missing piece to the positive thinking conversation is that there is a component of karma or God's will. Mother Gavrielia, the Greek Orthodox nun, says that whatever happens is because God wills it or God allows it. Either way, it is the best thing for your soul. That is difficult, especially when children are chronically or fatally sick. I like the idea that we raised our hands before we came down this lifetime and agreed to certain soul contracts and certain dramas to better our souls. Did I have a soul contract with my first husband? Is he the one who taught me resilience and creativity in a tight corner? What about my daughter who died an hour after birth? Do I have a soul contract with Mary Rose to further open my shattered heart? Today my son tells me that he wants to send a deeply pink rose from the Botanical Gardens to his sister in heaven. *I will send it to her and then she will get it,* he says. I turn my face away in tears. Did my son have any thoughts that brought upon his sister's death and this loneliness we have for the one we love?

Elizabeth Harper's book is balanced because even though she gives us the means to wish or pray for a better life, she does not blame anyone for illnesses. Harper writes,

> We are so quick, especially in this New Age society, to think we are to blame for illness. We are not. It may be part of the package deal of this life, or it could be a "contract," as medical intuitive Caroline Myss likes to call it. Whatever it is, illness

is there to show us something about ourselves that can be revealed through that suffering. It may also be the only way for us to bring some part of ourselves to the surface (158).

She continues with a partial list of "deeper motivations behind illness," including the connections that our situation gives us with others. After an illness or trauma, we are able to help others in a way that we could not before. As Arielle Greenberg writes in *Home/Birth: a poemic*, co-written with Rachel Zucker, about her stillborn son, Day,

> I never thought I would be writing this. I never thought this would be my story.
> But it is, so I tell people, and hold this space (195).

We can each hold the space for our suffering and for those who suffer around us. We can hold the space for the aunt diagnosed with meningioma or the mother diagnosed with ALS.

I've been listening to Krista Tippett's podcast *On Being*. Again and again her guests talk about suffering. Sharon Salzberg says that everyone suffers on earth. We cannot avoid suffering as humans. She discusses that the way we respond to the suffering is what varies. How gracefully do we walk through our parents' aging, our friend's suicide, another death? The human condition is preponderant on suffering. We are born in the trauma of labor, born after a long journey from a safe watery place through the canal that brings us to the light and darkness of this earth. I see suffering around me, and I want to hold people in my arms and tell them that it is okay. We are in this together. I want people to stop blaming each other when difficulties come. Perhaps it was my fault I lived in poverty with a mentally ill person as long as I did. I stayed, didn't I? But until that veil was lifted from my eyes, I could not see clearly. I could not believe that a husband would lie every day to his wife. I could not believe that someone would pretend to have a job. But I learned a lot there, and now after walking through my daughter's pregnancy and death, and that sharp grief afterwards, I can say that we each have certain things that we must suffer in this life. I am of Greek descent after all, and we do believe in Fate.

If God allows us some suffering, then He also allows the way through it. I believe in being positive, but I also believe in anger and sadness and rage. And when we harness those darker emotions, and lead them to the Light within, they are transmuted into joy, and we become stronger. For those who continue to preach that 100% of everything that happens to us is born of our thoughts, I think about gardens growing and abundance, but even the cucumber plant withers after she bears her fruit. I am at the point in my life when I am ready to accept my broken humanity: my frailties, constitution and life. I hope that I can be grateful each day as I was on the day my daughter was born and died. When Grace said to Mary Rose, *Open up your eyes, Baby Girl, and look at your mama,* she did. Mary Rose opened up her eyes, and I saw that they were blue. Not everyone who carries a baby with trisomy 18 gets to see her child's eyes. I am blessed. And Mother Gavrielia is right. Mary Rose is so very good for my soul.

The Grief of Siblings

MY SON SAYS TO ME, *Mommy, I want to die. I want to go to heaven to see my sister, Mary Rose. I miss my sister.* My son was almost two and a half when he embraced and kissed his newborn sister. Father John took Mary Rose's body to the church when my son was asleep. When he woke up the next morning he asked me, *Where is my sister? Where is Mary Rose?* We talk about the grief of mothers and fathers, but siblings have grief to bear without the understanding that adults have about death. If we have trouble processing the death of a loved one, what is it like for our little ones who are grappling with the reality of death?

I've only been to the cemetery once since Mary Rose's funeral on August 9. We did not bring our son to the funeral, though he was introduced to his sister and encouraged to be with her in the short time that we were together as a family on the earth plane. Before we went to the cemetery to see her stone in February, I explained to my son that we have a soul and a body. I told him an angel takes the soul up to heaven and that Mary Rose was given a new body with no owies, that heaven is a place where everyone is together with God, but it gets confusing because I also tell him that his sister is here with us, and that God is everywhere. When we went to the cemetery on a Sunday morning, my son was excited when he got out of the car. He looked around frowning at the stone markers and asked, *Where is my sister?* Apparently my discussion of laying the body to rest didn't do much for my then three-year-old son.

I know that many people bring small gifts to their family members' gravesites and go often, speaking to their loved ones there, feeling comforted. The cemetery is an important part of many people's healing. Mary Potter Kenyon writes beautifully about her visits to her husband's grave in her book *Refined by Fire: A Journey of Grief and Grace.* Her husband died unexpectedly. I wonder if it is different when people expect a loved one to die. Perhaps for those of us who know that death is coming, the cemetery is not as essential because we start grieving with the diagnosis. We brought crystal angels and hearts to the cemetery and placed them on Mary Rose's stone, but I left feeling bereft. My son seemed troubled too.

How can I go to heaven? my son asks again. *Can I take a plane? Can I take a train?* I remind him of the angel that is our transportation to heaven, and he stares at me, trying to figure this out. *I don't want to stay on earth any more*, he says, *I want to be with my sister.*

There are several children's books on death and I have read a few, though I hesitate to show them to my son. Many of these books talk about a final good-bye, focusing on the finality of death. For those of us who don't believe that the relationship with our loved one ends with death, how can we explain the transition of the soul from one life to the next? I continue to love my aunt, Matina; my grandmother, Despina; my daughter, Mary Rose. I feel them. They come to me in my dreams. I hear them whispering through the breeze. There is no end to my relationship with them, and love continues to grow. I know that for those who don't believe in the afterlife, this might seem strange, but I never thought that this was it. Each life touches one person and then another and another and continues after death through us and through the expansive life of the soul which never ends.

I recently enrolled my son in a grief program called The Healing Chickadee, offered by founder Terry Murphy through wordbirddelivers.com. Ms. Murphy's brother died when she was a little girl, and she did not have the language or tools to explore her grief and process her great sadness. My son will receive a bird each month with a story and lesson that deals with grief. We received DeeDee first, the chickadee whose grandmother died. She comes with a cardboard birdhouse to paint and decorate. We love DeeDee. After we received her, my son asked, *Mommy are you too old? Are you old enough to die?* I tell him that most people die when they are old, and I remind him how old his great-grandmother is. I tell him that only God knows when people will die. I am honest because I want him to know the truth: that life is messy and chaotic and that death comes to every family.

For the siblings who have their own trauma, it is important to talk about the emotions that come up as the children are ready. My son seems very shaken when he sees newborns. After a pediatrician's visit where he saw a newborn in the waiting room, my son says, *Our Mary Rose didn't move. Our Mary Rose didn't cry.* The first time he saw a newborn move her arms, he was startled. His sister could not move from her weak muscles, and then she was still, wrapped in a pink blanket that said Mary Rose.

Sometimes my son says, *Mommy, I want a baby in our house. Two babies.* Other times he says, *Mommy, all your babies will die. If God gives us another baby, it will die too.* I imagine that if there is another pregnancy, it will bring up trauma for my son, remembering me weeping for months, limping in back pain. I will hold his hand and snuggle and tell him that God is in charge, that every life does what it is supposed to do; for a minute or an hour or several decades, each life has a purpose.

In the Orthodox Christian liturgy we pray for the living and the dead at each service. Somewhere in the hymns and prayers and communion with one another we find that we are all connected and united in Christ. Christ means Light. If we make the choice, we too can embody Light. The holy doors to the altar of the temple or church stand between heaven and earth in the iconography depicted. On the one side we see Mary, the *Theotokos*, God-bearer, holding her son, and on the other side, Christ, the *Pantocrator*, who will come again, according to our traditions and scriptures. If we are honest, we live between heaven and earth, between the ancestors and the future generations. The Native Americans believe that a laboring woman stands between death and life, as the veil thins to allow each soul to enter from one world into the other. I too am a door between heaven and earth. I walk holding my son's hand, and I feel Mary Rose with us.

Sometimes I wonder if our family will always grieve Mary Rose. There are moments of such sharp grief of missing her, I know that I will miss her my entire life. I am grateful for the opportunity to nurture her in my body, to be the opening through which she came. Birth work is sacred work. Our grief is also sacred, especially the grieving of our young children. As their parents, we can honor their path as they love and miss their siblings. We walk together, taking another step forward on this meandering road.

Mother's Day

I REMEMBER MOTHER'S DAY ONE YEAR AGO when I was surprised by the intensity of my grief. It had been two months since Mary Rose's diagnosis. I was almost seven months pregnant. She moved inside me; her motions and limbs were tiny. I remember crying outside, sitting on my green garden chair. I cried all day because I knew that this would be our only Mother's Day physically together. This year is different. I'm just starting to come out of more than a year-long daze of shock and grief. I want to tell every mother whose child is gone through miscarriage or illness or accident, *Cry. You have earned the right to cry.* Well-meaning people tell us not to show our emotions, but we don't have to hide the intensity of our path.

My dear friend, Daniela, crocheted a rose with Mary Rose's name on the back and sent it for Mother's Day. It is the first gift that I have received honoring my daughter that hasn't sent me into fits of weeping. It still stings to see a joyful, pregnant woman or a newborn girl. Doing family things and witnessing children growing and playing and being alive often still hurts, especially the children born around the same time as Mary Rose. The first holidays after Mary Rose died were almost unbearable, except I'm still here.

Mother's Day is a tough holiday. It excludes many people. For women who are infertile and childless (not by choice), it is a reminder of what they do not have. For people whose mothers are on the other side of the veil, there is a void, and for those of us whose children have died, what do we do with this rosy, cheery, pastel pink holiday? I've been thinking of Louisa all week. Her mother and only son are on the other side of the veil, yet she meditates and lives her life with a vivacious grace that inspires me.

Louisa and I have both connected with the spirits of our children through prayer and meditation. We feel them close by and know that they are now intercessors, spirit guides and helpers, depending on the language we use. This year I propose that instead of listening to our sad thoughts, that we are separate from the ones who have died, let's think with our hearts. Our children's souls are intact and, if we think with our heart centers, reality shifts from a thinking place of lonely loss to a heart place of loving communion. This year I invite each of you whose children or mothers are not in an earthly body to light a candle and celebrate anyway. It is my great hope that we can celebrate this Mother's Day with tearful smiles and an understanding that the veil is thin, that our loved ones speak to us and send us messages of love from their heavenly place.

I have been listening to Kari Samuels' *28 Days of Angel Meditations* this month. When she says *Archangel Gabriel, please come*, I feel such peace. I choose to say *Mary Rose, come*, and Louisa chooses to say *Colin, come*. We are not separate from our children who continue to live through us and with us.

I am married to a man who is very sensible and practical, and he's married to a former English major who sees symbolism everywhere. I carry feathers into the house proclaiming that they are signs from my daughter saying that she loves me. He tells me that birds molt. On New Year's Day I found a heart-shaped rock in the middle of a brick outside. I had asked Mary Rose for a sign that she would still be with me in 2015, the first full year without her earthly presence. *Coincidence*, my husband says, but I believe that these gifts come from our daughter.

This spring my husband turned the grill on under a flowering dogwood tree. One petal landed in the middle of his big hand, and he said it looked like a heart and he thought of Mary Rose. He said that all the dogwood petals looked like hearts this year.

I wish for each of you to find hearts and roses and feathers this Mother's Day, because our dear children are still our children. The Mother's Day gifts that we receive cannot be found in a Hallmark store.

Come, Sweet Child, Sweet Mother, Aunt, come, this Mother's Day and show us the truth about Life.

Why Do People Compare Grief?

I PULL INTO MY FRIEND'S DRIVEWAY at the end of the road and feel like I am visiting a magical place. I am thinking of fairies and woodland creatures as I get out of the car, taking in the shady property surrounded by pine trees and gardens with echinacea. I read about this house in Terry Jones-Brady's book *A Mosaic Heart: Reshaping the Shards of a Shattered Life.* Terry writes about her two daughters who both died of cystic fibrosis and her first husband's suicide five years later. She is outside waiting and asks me, *How long has it been?* I pause, surprised that it is June 8. It is ten months since I held my baby girl in my arms.

Terry and I have been talking about how people compare grief. The first time I met her in the fall, I muttered something about how my grief can't be compared to hers. *Grief is grief,* she said, *You can't compare.* Right then, in the wake of my new journey as a grieving mother, I saw my own conditioning. As a young child I was compared to other children and to my sister. We are taught to measure our achievements by looking at how others have done. We compare our paychecks, houses, cars, bodies, health and relationships to those of our relatives, co-workers and Facebook friends. We never know what goes on in someone else's house or heart when the lights go out, when we aren't there. Here in the club of parents whose children have died, how does it serve us to compare our grief? Who wins if one of us has more pain?

I think back to the many grant proposals I wrote and how we developed assessment tools to measure success. But can we measure or quantify grief? People try to do so. My mother tells me that my grief over burying my newborn, Mary Rose, is not as bad as the grief of her friends Judy and Steve, because their first daughter, Hannah Audrey, died at 18 months of brain cancer. Judy and Steve's pain is not as deep as Miko's grief. Her son, Josh, was in his early twenties when he died suddenly in a car accident. Miscarried children aren't weighed on this scale most of the time. When I ask my mother how she came up with her statements, she says that when you have more memories, you miss the child more. According to this scale, the longer a child lives, the deeper the grief.

I disagree. I think of my daughter's life and I try to extrapolate a new memory, a part of her, something from our journey. I had contractions for the duration of her life. She was buried in her baptismal gown though there was no baptism. No milestones. No smiles. It was one life-changing moment. Sometimes I only remember the feeling of her weight in my arms wrapped in a blanket, my thought, *I can't believe it's already over,* and my son bending happily to give his beloved, still sister one more kiss. When I hear parents speak of their children who have reposed, they smile, often with tears in their eyes, remembering outings, moments, words, hugs, dreams and kisses. My heart longs to know something of my daughter's personality and quirks. I feel her presence with me, but my body and heart want more.

A couple of weeks ago Terry emailed a few friends about a negative Facebook experience. A friend told her that she should get over her daughters' deaths because Terry's grief was not one-tenth of her grief. This woman who had suffered abuse took to cyber-bullying a friend whose entire immediate family had died. Another friend who is a priest told Terry that losing a parish entailed more grief than losing a child. When Terry asked why, the response was, *Because God is in the parish.* Terry asks me, *Isn't God in a mother who bears her child?*

People tell me often that I shouldn't cry because I have a living son. I am reminded again and again that some people's first pregnancies end in death. Though I know that my son is a blessing, grief doesn't work that way. I carried and buried a child. I have a right to stay in the space of grief, to work through it, to feel the pain of not having my daughter here in the flesh for the rest of my life. She surrounds me. She is in my heart. I love her, but it still hurts.

Even in this essay discussing Mary Rose and Terry's beautiful daughters, Heather and Holly, let's not compare. A wise person said that comparison is violence toward God, who creates each of us with tender love. If we are all created in God's image, then how is one of us better than another? How does one person's grief hurt less? If we believe in soul contracts, fate, karma and God's will, then the tragedies of our lives shape us and prepare us for furthering our work on the planet. I believe that I was chosen to be Mary Rose's mother. Terry's path is different from mine, and so is her journey of grief. How could I compare a newborn, a 12-year-old and a 22-year-old daughter or how much their mothers miss them?

Terry made mosaics from broken pieces of Christmas ornaments and dishes and glass to process her grief. Some broke on their own, and she shattered others, arranging them to make beautiful art. One mosaic is on the cover of Terry's book. It has several word fragments: *glad, tidings, herald, Child's, Earth, world, Joy, Peace.* John Milton's words, *But what is strength without a double share of wisdom,* appear unbroken, and the angel, whose left hand and wings are missing, looks out at us, her chin held high.

The Power of Mourning

THIS JULY MY HUSBAND AND I took two nights to go away without our son. We became pregnant soon after we met, and our life together has been about being parents. Tim and I walked along the small town of Greenport in Long Island, New York. No Starbucks. No Home Depot. These old North Fork towns are still quaint, in part because there is no space to build up a Route 1 or Post Road. We visited our dear friend, Vivian, walked to an old lighthouse built in the 1800s, had coffee in a family-owned café and walked along the rocky beach, gathering stones and shells to bring back to our son. The sun was setting as we walked holding hands, and I thought about last summer. I didn't think that I would be married for long after Mary Rose died.

My husband and I had very different responses to our grief over Mary Rose's condition and death. There was no place where I could step away from the reality of trisomy 18. I could not separate my body from Mary Rose and, once she was born, my postpartum body physically wanted its newborn. I have never grieved so physically for so long. My husband has a good and open heart, but he is able to compartmentalize and stay busy. Tim tried to ignore Mary Rose's diagnosis before she was born. I handled most of the medical and birth planning. Where I was nearly paralyzed by shock after Mary Rose died, my husband stayed home from work for one week and then got busy. I needed to feel my pain, but he opened himself up to his grief in smaller increments. My husband grieves his daughter's brief life and death, but he isn't going to write a poem or make a painting to process that grief. Men and women are different, and we walked through our initial mourning alone, handling each moment the best way that we could. As my grief mellowed a bit, and he processed some of his grief, we have caught up as a couple. I lived through what I hope was the hardest year of my life, and my marriage is intact. Perhaps it is stronger for the wear and tear of such emotional challenges.

Before heading back to Virginia, I took my husband to the Hudson River town, Cold Spring. We walked into the art gallery, Studio 66 NY, and met the artist, Maureen Winzig, whose painting, *Manifest*, caught my attention. In the caption next to the painting Ms. Winzig writes,

> Power is so subjective. There is power in being illusive, in mourning, in dreaming. . . . Women and men have their own unique kinds of power. In this series I have chosen to express my thoughts on "Finding Power: Women of Courage, Passion, and Character" in ways that may be overlooked. . . . Women take on the grief of mourning and cleansing the soul and then find the strength to pray for the world and manifest an energy that bursts out from within that most powerful feminine core. . . .

In the painting the woman stands in her light, which is radiated in all directions. Her light is overtaking the darkness, but the darkness is still there in the background. Her posture is one of openness and expansion. Her chin is lifted up as if she is in a power pose. Her chest and shoulders are open. This is a determined woman who knows darkness and light. When I read Ms. Winzig's words, I thought about the power of mourning. Are those of us whose babies have died that woman? Could our words and light be illuminating for others going through dark times?

This last year has been about walking through inexplicable grief, experiencing the uncomfortable feelings and emotions that came up, many of them from other times in my life. Mary Rose brought up every fear I've ever had. Therapy has been vital as we talked and analyzed and blessed many challenges and traumas, working through the grief as it manifested. Am I more powerful for mourning and allowing my vulnerability to show, creating a space to paint and draw and write about my path?

After Mary Rose died, life continued. A friend was diagnosed with cancer. The young godson of a Facebook friend died of leukemia. Many healthy babies were born, and still more friends are pregnant. My sister moved to another state with her family. Her friend who suffered many miscarriages birthed a healthy girl in her 40s.

It is almost August 8, the one-year anniversary of my beloved daughter's birth and death. I am whole even as I am aware of my brokenness. This coming Sunday we will offer a memorial service for Mary Rose. I will bake a loaf of bread in the Syrian tradition, and Father James will read the prayers that my people have read for their ancestors' souls since the early days of Christianity and, actually before that, in the Judaic tradition. But in this time of remembrance, my friend Daniela is coming for a visit, and we plan a vacation to be with my sister and her family. The planet continues to turn and our feet are planted on Earth, roots deepening with each experience.

I am broken and whole.

There is power in mourning. The power comes from lassoing intense grief, which comes from deep love, to fuel our internal Light. Sometimes all we have is a flickering and sputtering spark in our heart center. The spark unites us to Creator and each other, eventually shimmering brightly again if we allow the space for the love called mourning.

The Christ Heart Meditation

I MEDITATE ONE NIGHT, unable to sleep once again, tears in my eyes, hands on my pregnant womb, when I merge with Christ's heart for a few moments. I wiggle and I squirm. Meditation is not my strongest skill, but I continue to sit on my purple cushion and breathe. I feel electrically connected to everyone in a web of golden Light. There is a charge in the connection. Total Peace. I will be okay if my baby dies. My heart expands in love and light and unity. I am one pregnant woman who will bury her baby, but I am loved and there is mercy being showered into every cell of my being, my baby's being, into the depths of my soul. In the center of Christ's heart I am loved and whole, one small part of a bigger work of creation.

Are you ready to try this?

Close your eyes and get into a comfortable seated position. Take a few deep breaths. Relax your body. Imagine sitting behind Christ who is also in the same seated position. Merge your heart with His heart. Enter Him through His heart. You are one with Christ. You are completely surrounded by Christ and His Light. Take deep breaths and feel this energy of deep peace. You might see certain colors or hear the refrain of a special song or hymn. Continue to take deep breaths and feel Christ's energy. Feel your place and connection to everyone and everything in the Universe. Breathe in peace and acceptance. Christ accepts you as you are. Please accept yourself as you are. Forgive yourself as you are forgiven by God. Stay here as long as you like, allowing your heart to be showered with love and light. When you are ready, open your eyes and wiggle your toes and fingers before getting up.

I will meet you at the center of Christ's heart.

Social Media and Grief

It is July 2014. I am pregnant with a baby who is dying. I wait and wait. Each day and night is long and feels like a week. I sit inside most of the summer, unable to be active because of pain in my hips and legs and back. I am on my computer where, if I cry, no one will know. A Facebook friend, who is also a midwife, posts "I hate all things postpartum." She has just given birth to a beautiful healthy son, her second living child. I feel like someone has slapped me in the face. The words sting, and they stay with me for a long time. I know that she does not hate her beautiful newborn son.

Other Facebook friends complain about their pregnancies. They are uncomfortable or the baby is big and active and kicks once again. I remember how much I wished my daughter would move and grow, how much I wanted a normal pregnancy with kicking and turning. Instead, I carried a baby who barely moved, and I planned her funeral, praying that I would meet her alive, even for a moment. After an ectopic pregnancy, my sister listened to her pregnant co-worker complain about the sacrifice of not drinking for nine months. An infertile friend tells me that she is tired of hearing her pregnant friends complain about the nausea and kicking when she longs to carry a child.

There are many of us hurting, while others seem to take for granted the good fortune of their healthy pregnancies and healthy children. I was childless for 15 years, and I remember that constant discussion point around the question, *Do you have children?* I could not understand then, and I still do not understand, why this role of motherhood is one that should define us. I was a writer, a grant writer, a teacher, a poetry therapist, but none of that came up in conversations. There is no need to ask a woman if she is a mother. She will tell you about her children even if you don't ask.

One in four pregnancies ends in miscarriage and one in 160 births is still. A certain percentage of newborns and babies die from neonatal illnesses and SIDS, and another percentage of women are infertile. Many of us hold our electronic devices looking at ultrasound photos, birth announcements, and the joys and the complaints of parenthood. How do we take the posts and life trajectories of our friends and colleagues who seem to be clueless about other people's struggles? They might not mean any harm by their posts, but somehow those words and photos hurt our broken hearts. Pictures of newborns, especially girls, still sting. I bless each baby I see, and remember my sweet Mary Rose, longing to hold her in my arms.

I didn't know that my friend Yana was pregnant at Mary Rose's funeral. She didn't tell me for a few months, and she never announced her pregnancy on Facebook. She refused to post ultrasound photos. Yana is an academic whose first two pregnancies ended prematurely. Many women work well into their forties, putting family on hold until they are established in their field, and sometimes it is too late to conceive. We discussed Facebook and she said, *I won't put this on Facebook because I do not know who is looking and who is suffering in her own situation.* Perhaps only those of us who have been on the other side of the normal and exhausting joys of parenthood are aware of the pain and emptiness within a woman who wants to hold a living child in her arms.

The way that I have handled social media is either to hide or unfriend anyone who is causing me any disturbance in my inner peace. I don't think that people who have hundreds of friends but are only acquaintances of mine will notice when I click "Unfriend." And for those who are closer to me, who might have some interest in my own life, I click "Unfollow." I don't want to read angry or upsetting posts. I know that my deep and meaningful relationships are alive in person, on the phone and on Skype.

I know people who have deactivated their Facebook accounts, but I am grateful to my trisomy 18 community and support system that has linked me to other women going through their grieving process. It was in Facebook messages that I got to know my friend Sindy, who painted "Healing Companion." I became friends with a dear woman and artist from California, Lakshmi, whose son Siddha was born and died the April before Mary Rose. I also came to know a woman, Sherri, whose last two pregnancies ended in death due to trisomy 18. Her sons are named Bryson and Ryder. I love these women, though I have never met them in person. Their babies are in my hearts.

One of my friends recently had a grief-related, cyber-bullying experience with one of her Facebook friends, and I encouraged her to stay connected online and recognize that she has control over some of the experience by unfriending and un-following people who are challenging. There are many who look at the dangers of the Internet, but if we use this virtual world to support and encourage each other, then we can use it for good. Most of my support came through a screen, as I did not get out much during my pregnancy. I hated the phone during those many long months and am only returning calls recently. I could not control my weeping, and I can't talk while I cry. The phone seemed useless to me after finding out about Mary Rose's genetic defect. One of my dearest friends, Paige, thought I was upset with her when I didn't return her calls last spring. I started to cry on the phone thinking that I had hurt my friend. Every word took such effort, and I did not know what would trigger my tears.

It is my hope that we can be more sensitive to our others: our friends, relatives, bosses, sisters, acquaintances and women who are each walking and maneuvering through their own personal challenges. I don't have too many answers, but I'm willing to discuss ways that we can become more sensitive to each other's path. I'm certain that we can make this easier together, by considering the weight of our words and actions, even our inactions. We are connected on the web and in life. Let's connect our hearts and consider those who are suffering quietly, watching and reading our words through a screen with tears in their eyes.

Another Child?

I HANG UP MY SKYPE CALL to my therapist and see that NPR has a story on new studies that link higher autism rates to older parents, specifically mothers over 40 and fathers over 50. They do not mention the rates for 48-year-old fathers. I prom-ised myself a year to work through my grief before I decide yes or no to another pregnancy, and that year is coming to a close. I am almost 43 years old. My first two pregnancies were unplanned, but now I am in a different position. I imagine a healthy baby in our house so that my tender son can grow up with a living sibling. But I now know many things that I wish I could unknow. It isn't just trisomies that concern me; there are many other defects and illnesses that I had never heard of be-fore. And of course there are the usual worries, such as miscarriage, SIDS and in-creasing rates of many chronic childhood disorders.

Most grief books about baby death discuss a subsequent pregnancy. Some peo-ple get pregnant right away, thinking that this will take away the pain of their pre-vious pregnancy, though it does not. One baby cannot erase the pain of missing another baby who has died. Others choose never to have another pregnancy, never to take a chance on another baby having the same disorder or defects. Some parents decide to adopt, and several people have suggested that to me. Adoption takes advocacy, and I'm burnt out after taking care of my terminally ill aunt and fighting to give my daughter a quiet home birth. At 43 I have a 95% chance of having a child without trisomy 18, 13 or 21. I am a worrier by nature. After a pregnancy that ends in death, what comes next?

My friend Yana has a daughter who needs a liver transplant. Her daughter is two years old now and will probably have the surgery in a couple of years. Yana and her husband each carry the gene for Crigler-Najjar syndrome. Each of their pregnancies brings a 25% chance of this disorder. They asked themselves if they could handle another child with this disease and they decided that they could. They just birthed a healthy baby girl. My friend Terry, on the other hand, gave birth to two daughters with cystic fibrosis and they both died. She also had a 25% chance of this illness with each pregnancy. Terry does not regret her children, nor, when her doctor suggested an abortion during her second pregnancy, did she ever wish that she had made a different choice. Mary Rose's trisomy 18 was a random defect. The rates go up slightly as women get older. There was over a 2% chance of having a child with trisomy 18 at 42 years of age.

Sometimes I repeat Byron Katie's words "I want whatever God wants" (Yacaboni, 73), and mean them with all of my being. There are moments when I know that no matter what I choose or what I do, I will be all right. After Mary Rose's death I told my therapist how scared I was that my son would die too. We looked at that fear, and I realized that if that happened, somehow I could survive that too. Look in the cracks of the sidewalk and see how life seeds itself and grows in unlikely places.

I am thinking of Stanley Kunitz's poem "Touch Me," where he writes about his garden and crickets and asks,

What makes the engine go?

Desire, desire, desire

The longing for the dance
stirs in the buried life (158).

What are my desires? Do I desire another pregnancy to heal this one? To end my childbearing years on a different note? And then I remember Jean Valentine's poem "The River at Wolf," where she reminds me,

Blessed are they who remember
that what they now have they once longed for (25).

What do I long for now? A healthy baby in my arms? Could I handle another Mary Rose? A child with another illness, severe or not? Would I ever regret the outcomes of another pregnancy? It is almost time to answer these questions. I do not know what the next few months or years will bring, but I know that I agree with Byron Katie about something else. She says that life breathes us, that if we don't have the answer yet, then it isn't time to make a decision. Katie says that when the decision has to be made, it makes itself. So I am waiting just a little bit longer to see what that decision might be.

Krista Tippett interviewed Jean Vanier, founder of L'Arche, on her radio program, *On Being*. He talks about the communities that he founded for people with disabilities and about the "equilibrium of the heart." Vanier finds that when you open your heart to be present to people considered ugly and broken, you find peace. There, among the dark places of our illnesses, we find peace and, therefore, God. He tells a story about St. Francis and how he disliked lepers. St. Francis said, "One day the Lord brought me to the lepers and when I left, there was a new gentleness in my body and in my spirit. From there I really left to serve the Lord." What is it inside of us that turns away from people with disabilities and illnesses? Even St. Francis had trouble with the lepers of his time. When my aunt was paralyzed in her hospital bed, swollen from steroids, friends and relatives said, *I can't look at her like that*, and some stopped visiting. I looked at her and touched her. I brought my son to her as an offering, and he kissed her and played on her hospital bed amidst the body that could no longer do what she wished it to do.

And my daughter, my six-pound baby, who could only open one eye, whose head was too big, chin too small, feet too long, whose muscles had no tone at all and whose limbs splayed – I held that child and loved her in the murky waters of her birth. I told her that she could go to her heavenly place, that we would be okay. My husband, son, mother, midwives, doula and two friends were in that space of a failing newborn's body, and we were all changed. How could I not find God holding my daughter with severe developmental disabilities and defects across her whole body? How could I not find peace? Those who opened their hearts to Mary Rose saw a glimmer of God and holiness. Those who chose to ignore her existence were not open to the "equilibrium of the heart." By closing our eyes and our hearts to the darker parts of humanity, we are denying ourselves the love that fills our broken and cracked hearts. It seems that the more we are broken, the greater our capacity to be present in the moment and to love unconditionally.

My dear homeopath is nervous about pregnancies in women over 40. I don't ask her why, but I imagine that she has formed her belief over her research studies and her private practice. The high-risk ob/gyn I saw during my pregnancy with Mary Rose smiled and said, *You should definitely try again. Most of my patients are infertile*. She highly doubted that another pregnancy with such complications would be our lot. My midwife, Grace, thinks getting pregnant again is a great idea, the sooner the better. She thinks that the data are distorted, as fewer women give birth in their 40s and so the numbers are off. Grace has also sent me some recent studies that indicate that women in their 40s have healthier outcomes because they take better care of themselves than younger mothers.

I imagine a room of 100 babies, my 100%. I walk in and look around. I want whatever God wants. Five of these babies have trisomies. At least three of them will die. The first few times I imagine this room of babies I am scared. Which are the five that I don't want? But then my heart softens, and I realize that I could love each of them. I don't know if I will become pregnant again or if I get to keep another child, nor do I know which one might be birthed. But I walk forward with trust in my heart. Whatever condition a baby is in, I can love her. I won't live by data and statistics alone. It is the heart, the heart that carries me forward, closer to the Light.

The Miscarriages

IT IS JULY, ALMOST THE ONE-YEAR milestone of August 8. It is my birthday. I am 43. I've been thinking about another child since my pregnancy with Mary Rose, but I am scared. And then my cycle is late. I am pregnant.

The surprise is that I am hopeful. I realize that the child already has her DNA in place. Mary Rose had trisomy 18 from conception. My husband is excited. We feel lucky that we can get pregnant again. Then I sense that something isn't right. My breasts aren't tender. My sense of smell is not sensitive like my other pregnancies. Three weeks later I miscarry. I bury the membrane under the statue of Our Lady of Guadalupe outside.

Now I know about this grief too. I am grateful that this didn't happen at 12 weeks or 16 weeks. I approach the anniversary of my daughter's death with a new death, another loss. Three pregnancies and one living child.

It is October and I am pregnant again. This time my hormones rage. It is Sunday, and I wake up after two dreams. I start bleeding in one dream. In the other dream my infertile friend, Paula, has a son. I text Paula that morning, and she replies, *It is a miracle*! She prayed to St. Anna, Mary's mother, and holds a positive pregnancy test in her hands reading my words. I miscarry later that day. Paula tells me that she has the same due date that I had.

I am furious. I rant. I weep. This was my last chance to birth at 43. The numbers for trisomies go up now. I decide that I never want to be pregnant again. I mope. I tell my therapist, *Four pregnancies and one living child.*

Now what? I find myself back on my meditation cushion and see Christ put His hand on my head. He says, *May your mind be Light. May your mind be Light. May your mind be Light.* Again and again. *May my mind be Light.*

I throw the dried roses from my blessingway into the compost. I separate Mary Rose from Mary Rose's sad pregnancy. I do not know what comes next, but I bless my body and know now that if there is another pregnancy there are no guarantees or certainties. Before these miscarriages I assumed that I would get pregnant again and carry to term. I worried about infant death and genetic illnesses, not miscarriage.

These two miscarriages have reset my womb and my mind. I no longer know that there will be another living child.

Halloween

IT IS THE SECOND HALLOWEEN without my baby girl. I have been thinking all day about my Facebook feed with pictures of adorable children in their Halloween costumes. I love these pictures. I enjoy seeing my friends' children, my niece and nephew and cousins. But today I did not post a picture of my son in his Martin Kratt bat creature power suit. He gives me his three-year-old stink face smile and I snap another photo. He holds my hand as we walk and trick-or-treat for the first time. We ring four doorbells, and he is in awe of the bowls full of candy. I do not post a photo of my son today because I've been thinking about the mothers who have had miscarriages and stillborn babies and babies who died after birth. I am thinking of my friends struggling with infertility. My Facebook page is blank today because I am holding the space for the babies we love who aren't here.

Halloween isn't even a holiday, my husband says when I tell him what is on my mind. But Halloween is a part of our American culture. Tonight my pumpkins are in memory of the babies who are not here. I know that they are very close to us. In our hearts. On our minds. May our world remember us too: the mothers and fathers and siblings of children on the other side of the veil.

As night settles in around us, children shout, *Trick or Treat*! My son holds my hand and the jack-o-lantern's glow reminds me of my daughter, my love, my Light.

The Veils of Grief

AUTUMN IS MY FAVORITE SEASON. After the hot summer I look for naked trees and the simplicity that is winter. Our surroundings change as nature prepares to rest. Most of us keep up a fast pace through the holidays, but I like to walk at dusk and watch the light fade as if God has a dimmer switch. The silhouette of trees against a graying sky comforts me. In my poem "Winter Comes" from Marietta Bratton's anthology *I Will Bear This Scar: Poems of Childless Women*, I write, "I long for bare bone of tree. / Why can't my excess catch fire / and blow away becoming one with the wind" (86)? Somehow the bright and dull-colored leaves falling help me to process my past year. In the Orthodox Church, as well as in other traditions such as Judaism and Native American spirituality, the new year starts in September. It is a time of harvest and the start of the school year. It is a time that leads us to a more quiet place, a time of prayer and intention setting.

When I received the news that my baby had trisomy 18, it was March. I felt mocked by the leaves sprouting and those first yellow buds opening. I walked through spring and summer and five months of knowing that my baby would die, while life hummed and buzzed and blossomed all around me. My body was blooming too but I had a hard time processing my pregnancy. I walked one step at a time, tentatively moving forward hour by hour, day by day and then month by month, as I counted and recounted days and months, trying to measure the immeasurable.

In November I went to tour The Glass House in New Canaan, Connecticut, with a friend. It was Thanksgiving week and unseasonably warm. We met at the Visitors Center and took a shuttle to the home of architect Philip Johnson, now a historic site and museum. The leaves were mostly gone. After wanting to visit The Glass House for a few years, I was there at the close of the perfect exhibit for a grieving mother: *Fujiko Nakaya: Veil*. Nakaya uses fog as a sculptural medium. Our small group was standing outside The Glass House when the fog seemed to seep out of the foundation, enveloping the house, trees and landscape. Since the house is all glass, we could see through the fog into the house, and then outside the structure to the other side of the property. Layers of mist obscured our view, then lifted softly. I stood in the fog remembering Avalon and God and Mary Rose.

Grief descends like a misty veil and covers my sight and my view. It happened when my friend Jeanette took her life at 27 years old. It is happening now that Cubby has died. I no longer see what other people see. I view life through my own lens, which is now foggy. And then slowly the mist lifts a little and I catch a glimpse of something that I couldn't see before. In the case of this tour, I saw trees coming into view. I turned and could see the lake beyond the house. The veil descends and the veil lifts. Sometimes the veil rips us open; everything inside breaks and shifts. I will never see the world the way that I did before trisomy 18. And I have decided that this is more than fine. I can accept my new raw perception of life and death.

We suffer and then we choose how we will integrate our suffering. I hope, like Nakaya's exhibit, I can take my experience and make something beautiful. Winter comes. We too process and release our grief and excess. We too have bare bones like tree bark reaching up to the sky and the light. Even when the fog descends or ascends for a while I reach toward the setting sun and face my night with my eyes wide open.

Thanksgiving, Gratitude, Grief and a Book Review

ARTHUR C. BROOKS' OP-ED IN *The New York Times,* "Choose to be Grateful. It Will Make You Happier," cites research about gratitude and "greater life satisfaction." Gratitude stimulates the brain. He writes, "Choosing to focus on good things makes you feel better than focusing on bad things." This is something that most Americans agree with, but where do grieving mothers fit in? Is remembering our children who are no longer here a sign of ingratitude? Last night I read Angela Miller's post "Grateful and Grieving" from her blog *A Bed for My Heart*. She eloquently discusses her grief and how grieving is not a sign that we are not grateful. Miller writes, "It's not one *or* the other. Yes I'm *still* grieving because I love and miss my son with every molecule in my body, but that doesn't mean I'm not also deeply thankful for my blessings."

Recently my mother went to a family gathering and an aunt asked her, *Is Dianna still sad*? The answer is yes. Dianna is still sad. Others offer my mother advice for me. *It is time for Dianna to find closure. She needs to move on. She has a son.* One woman told me that I have to look at what I do have, not at what I don't have. I have a living son and a daughter on the other side of the veil.

Two years ago I was newly pregnant at Thanksgiving, feeling first-trimester sick. I was not thinking too much about the abstraction of who my baby would be. But I did think, *This is my second pregnancy. I'm done child-bearing after this.* I imagined that I would birth a healthy child. I imagined that all would be fine. Now, two years later, that assumption no longer exists. This year I prepare for the Thanksgiving holiday, and my heart still hurts.

Brooks' op-ed made me smile because I am grateful for many things, like this cold New York evening and red leaves almost gone from their tree. I am grateful for my family and for my friends. I am grateful for Mary Rose, but can I also be grateful for trisomy 18? Can I be grateful for the life that she was given? Her 42 weeks inside me, and one hour outside?

I was recently asked, *How old would she have been*? at a Mothers of Preschoolers (MOPS) meeting. My eyes opened wide because I stopped my brain from thinking those thoughts. I do not let myself think about how many months Mary Rose would be or what she would have been doing. In August my husband said, *She would have been walking.* And I turned to him and replied, *But she would not have been walking.* I cannot separate my daughter's body from trisomy 18. But I quickly did some math in my head that Wednesday morning and answered with tear-filled eyes, *She would have been 15 months old.* My friend Terry came for a visit on her daughter's birthday last week. We spoke about grief and life and anxiety and post-traumatic stress disorder and our children. *Heather would have been 46 today,* she said. Angela Miller writes about the empty chair "where my seven year old should be sitting." And here we are living in this world of juxtapositions and paradoxes. Of reality and imagination. Our children, who are always our children, are now ageless.

In Elizabeth McCracken's memoir, *An Exact Replica of a Figment of My Imagination*, she writes about her first son who was born still at 41-and a-half weeks. Her pregnancy was a happy time. There were no complications until he died in utero. McCracken stays on the practical, tangible side of her grief. She does not believe in God, which does not upset me, but when she speaks of her dead son, it is difficult for me to process death without the spiritual dimensions. McCracken is honest and talks about her travels, her pregnancy and her expectations for her son. Some of her insights are important, though I cannot relate to her decision not to take a photo of her son, or not to have her husband present at the delivery, or how instead of giving the boy one of the names that they picked out and were considering, they put Pudding on the death certificate, which was his nickname through the pregnancy. I chose a different path, but I appreciate McCracken's thoughtful exploration of her experience with her stillborn son.

In discussing her grief and other people's sympathy, McCracken writes that "grief lasts longer than sympathy, which is one of the tragedies of the grieving" (80). *Is that what this is?* The world moves so quickly around me, and people want me to stop talking about my daughter who died, even though she is still my daughter. I listen to them speak of their many living children. What negates my own daughter's existence? And yes, my heart is still tender and raw, and I do seek comfort. I want to make sense out of this trauma and grief, and I cannot do it alone. McCracken speaks about the social aspect of the grieving parent after mentioning her pregnancy or her stillborn son to others. She writes, "People changed the subject. They smiled uncomfortably. . . . They didn't mention it. They did not say, *I am so sorry* or *How are you?*" She goes on to discuss how surprised she was when people didn't mention her son or pregnancy (92). When I saw my uncle for the first time in over a year he did not mention my pregnancy or my daughter. Chit chat. Small talk. When someone asks how many children I have, I always mention Mary Rose. The person looks at me in horror. A dead child! How could I speak of it?

McCracken beautifully and honestly writes,

> I've done it myself, when meeting the grief-struck. . . . To mention it by name is
> to conjure it up, not the grief but the experience itself: the mother's suicide, the

brother's overdose, the multiple miscarriages. The sadder the news, the less likely people are to mention it. The moment I lost my innocence about such things, I saw how careless I'd been myself.

I don't even know what I would have wanted someone to say. Not: It will be better. Not: You don't think you'll live through this, but you will. Maybe: To-morrow you will spontaneously combust. Tomorrow, finally your misery will turn to wax and heat and you will burn and melt till nothing is left in your chair but a greasy, childless smudge. That might have comforted me (94).

I was speaking to my friend Jenn about this very thing. She says she doesn't want to bring up the dead baby at work because she does not want to upset the mother. But the mother is never going to forget the baby. We remember our children, living and dead, and for Jenn to tell her co-worker that she is thinking of her child, she would acknowledge the child's existence, which is what we want. We don't get the milestones, the parties, the graduations, the holidays, so can our world give us an acknowledgement of the existence of our children? This Thanksgiving can we open our hearts to be grateful for the living and the dead? Can we make space around our tables for the memories of our children and other loved ones who have passed away? We remember the grandparents and parents and aunts, but when it comes to the children, we do not want to speak their names. As McCracken says, "The dead don't need anything. The rest of us could use some company" (138).

There is one more thing that McCracken says that strikes a chord with me this holiday season. She speaks of her pregnancy to her second son, Gus, and says, "there was nothing in my life that was not bittersweet. Every piece of hope was tinged with sadness; every moment of relief was lit on the edges with worry.... Of course [Gus] does not erase his older brother's death" (183). So when we gather this holiday season, please don't chastise a grieving mother or father or sibling for not getting over it. Please don't insist that living children should fill the empty space of where the other child used to be. Let's offer kind words instead. There is no getting over the death of a child. Or anyone else for that matter. As Lucie Brock-Broido writes in her poem "Pyrrhic Victory" found in Kevin Young's anthology *The Art of Losing: Poems of Grief and Healing,* "Some grief is larger than my body is" (20). Certainly this grief is larger than a month or a year, even when we are grateful for so much.

Navigating through the Holiday Season after Infant Death: A Meditation on *Joy, Interrupted*

'TIS THE SEASON. For those of us who have experienced miscarriage, stillbirth and infant death, how do we walk through the holiday cheer? It is the season for Christmas cards and sparkly cookies, parties and gifts. It is also the time of year when, somehow, the fact that the world keeps spinning without slowing down to acknowledge Mary Rose makes my heart feel a little more tender. This second year of holidays after my daughter's death from trisomy 18 hurts. After two early miscarriages in July and October, the holidays feel raw and holy. I walk this path gently.

My friend Daniela recently sent me the book *Joy, Interrupted,* edited by Melissa Miles McCarter. I love the title: *Joy, Interrupted.* Even in the midst of my pregnancy with Mary Rose, there were moments of joy. Snuggles and kisses. Loving conversations. Moments of grace when those who love me did stand by me. A bit of community. Hugs. I continue to find joy, even though it is interrupted by grief and longing.

In McCarter's book she collects works of various genres, including artwork. The editor's own daughter, Maddie, died at six weeks of SIDS. McCarter's pregnancy was not easy, and it ended for her in the death of her baby. She put together this anthology to heal and offer healing to others. The book has a range of topics including infertility, miscarriage, abortion, adoption, stillbirth, and infant and child death. The essays by Gabriella Burman about her daughter Michaela, who died suddenly at five years old, 12 days after her youngest daughter was born, brought tears to my eyes. Michaela, who had cerebral palsy, is a beautiful girl, and her eyes cut to my own heart. There are a few photos in the back of the book remembering those whom the writers honor.

Reading this collection during Advent, I pause to absorb the grief and stories in the anthology. I don't want to be swept up into the insanity of this season without remembering my family in its entirety. Last December I was in a foggy daze, but I wanted to create a good holiday for my living son. Through my tears and heartache, I decorated a tree, took a family photo, sent out cards and baked. But it hurt each step of the rocky path. People say that time makes this pain better. I am not quite as shocked this second holiday season without Mary Rose. I don't cry hysterically as often, but my eyes tear up frequently as I open my heart again and again. With each opportunity to love another, I open my heart to the chance of being broken again. I cannot build a fortress around my heart. As Marie Howe writes in her beautiful poem "What the Living Do," "I am living. I remember you" (90).

Last year when I worked on our family Christmas card I included Mary Rose's name after my son's name. The Armentrout family includes Mary Rose. Every time I sign a card from our family without her name, my heart aches. Perhaps I will change the wording on our Christmas card this year to say something like "and Mary Rose, in our hearts" or "and our intercessor, Mary Rose." Parents struggling to find their footing on how to be a family after infant loss can create a space to acknowledge all of their children.

Our friend Annie made us our Christmas stockings last year. She knitted these huge, beautiful, homemade stockings, and on the back there is an angel to remember Mary Rose. Mary Rose, whose only Christmas on Earth was that first year when I was newly pregnant with her. Isaiah's Promise sent a handmade pink stocking with Mary Rose's name on it and a small angel pin. This year I am thinking of putting something from Mary Rose to the other children in that stocking. If she is with us continuously and constantly, then what would be an appropriate gift to her brother and cousins? Chocolate? Perhaps this will be a new tradition for me to keep her in the family, to weave her short life here into our longer lives on this earth.

Two years ago, I bought a Christmas ornament from Brian Andreas and StoryPeople. It says,

I carry
you with
me into
the world,
into the smell of
rain & the words that
dance between people
& for me,
it will always
be this way,
walking in the light,
remembering being
alive together.

When I bought it I knew that my aunt would not live much longer. I unpacked the ornament last December after the year that changed everything. I wept because of the truth that now my daughter, that spark of life the previous December, was now somewhere else, not posing for photos under the tree, not growing, not here on this earth.

Last year my sister and her family made a donation to Isaiah's Promise for Christmas in memory of Mary Rose. This meant so much. Perhaps this holiday season for those readers who know of a family who has experienced a baby death, a small donation and a card with the name of the baby could be offered. It is the speaking of the name, the acknowledgment of the life that we mothers seek. The comfort is in coming together as a community to celebrate our living and our dead. We are intricately connected to the ancestors of different generations with their other-worldly presence.

As for the parties and the celebrations, I go to a few but give myself space to leave early or cry. I was at a meeting this week, and a tiny newborn girl with Mary Rose's coloring was right behind me, fussing as newborns do. I wanted to get up and leave, but I decided that I could make it through the two hours to be with my friends. Other times I just don't face the world because I can't. Cubby didn't go near babies for two years after her beloved newborn, Francis, died. I navigate the best I can and hope that each of you readers has good support, warm tea, and the space to rest and grieve in your own time. It is important to take the steps to rejoin the spinning world around us, but it is good to know one's own limitations too.

This year as I prepare for Christmas, I am in a different space. I think of the Christ child whom we remember this Christmas. I think of Mother Mary and how all mothers await their babies. I remember my anxious anticipation waiting for Mary Rose. A child is coming who promises peace and love to our broken world. Even in grief, the light settles in each day and a gerbera daisy blooms in December in my garden. When my aunt was suffering from atypical meningioma, Sister Evelyn of Mount St. Mary's Abbey told me to look for the small miracles that surround the difficult situation. Around my aunt's hospital bed many gathered. We shared chocolate. My son brought joy to her long days. She made us laugh until her very end. Indeed the miracles abound, but Sister Evelyn tells us to look for them. It's okay if our joy is interrupted by our grief, as long as we allow joy to come back again and again and again.

Part III

Poems and Fragments

Don't pity the mother
whose child drinks Light
instead of mother's milk.

Dianna Vagianos Armentrout

i stand on a precipice

of shattered glass

an angel hovers
    behind me

wind howls
in my ears

i lift up my arms
blood pulses

    my feet

sharp jagged shards
               fragments

Angel: one push.

she is transformed
for mary rose, august 2014

i walk to my daughter's grave
        the day after her birth
            (she isn't suffering)

my milk her milk   isn't leaking yet
        it will demand the newborn's open mouth

my breasts will ask *where is my baby?*
            again and again

i pick up a grey feather from the grass

                her soul soared out of her broken body

heal me now
        my angel, mother me

My Daughter, My Angel

My angel grew inside me until my womb swelled and my body opened. Then she surrounded me with wings and love. My daughter, Mary Rose, lived one sacred hour. I held her in my arms and had to let her go.

Why am I still here a month later when my body is heavy with grief and milk? How do I answer the question, *How many children do you have?* Dead babies and miscarriages are taboo in our society where positive thinking cures all. But this angel. . . .

Her energy is with me. I carry my daughter in my heart.

Mary Rose's portrait was painted months ago. In the painting I hold my pregnant belly and the angel holds me from behind. Her wings are my sanctuary. Prints of "Healing Companion" comfort mothers with infant losses. Now I write to heal myself and others. We women need each other to survive and bless this planet-in-transition. We are standing on stepping stones to higher consciousness. My heart is shattered and open. I will not hide my third-eye sight and intuition any more.

Mary Rose, bless us. Thank you for sending roses and feathers as you illuminate our path.

The Blessingway

After the blessingway
roses fall from my hair
white and pink – in each room of the house.

We dreamt of this as girls:
flowers braided into our hair.

The artist paints with henna
on my swollen belly:
roses and dragonfly
my skin loose this second time.

My daughter is dying inside me
her heartbeat strong inside me
where she is safe until labor

my womb the sacred space
between worlds: dark and light
contracting for 21 days.

All that, to hold her for a moment,
her broken heart and defects
body limp in my embrace, her blue eyes

and me in this pool as it fills with blood.
I hold her to me and whisper *We love you*
We love you, We'll always love you.

Go, I say, *do your work, Sweet Baby.*
The placenta is birthed and she slips away
so quietly I can't know the exact moment.

I carry her body wrapped in a blanket with pink roses
for hours, hungry and exhausted, I don't leave her
until that moment, the coffin on my bed.

Mother and I dress her in her christening gown
and lay her down, arms stiffening
body cooling. . . .

The Master asks *What now, Strong Woman?*
Then answers *Your milk will come in. You will awaken*
for weeks listening for cries never made.

And the child? I reply *The daughter?*
The one I longed for for decades?
—She does not desire one drop of your milk.

With the angels I still weep and cry
Holy, Holy. . . .

Their Bodies

At night my two-year-old says, *Mommy, come rest with me*
and I lay down on his bed touching his curly hair,
his body strong, his fingers perfect.

Mary Rose's fingernails were inverted
her body limp, defects throughout her form.

My body made one healthy boy and one broken girl.

I spoon my son and stroke his big feet
no baby between us now.

Sing *om bhur* he says, and I do, chanting the gayatri mantra
clutching his warmth which feels like fever after holding her.

Fragments

8/11/14

I am lost without you.
I listen for your cries
but you never cried.
You never drank
one drop of my milk.
My body pours out its rage
tear by tear, drop of milk by
                              drop

Where are you my Beloved?
How shall the heart be reconciled
to its feast of losses? *

8/21/14

Do I betray you by getting dressed?
Body healing, no longer stuck,
moving on.

No baby in my center.

No center.

I walk and cry.

September 2014

I miss my daughter.
I miss my Mary Rose.

10/31/14

What are these cellular memories made of?
          Salt and water, tears and love.

---

* From Stanley Kunitz's poem "The Layers."

March 2015

At the Statue of Our Lady of Guadalupe

Honor the ancestors
and you honor
          yourself.

Feed the ancestors
and you feed yourself.

Are we not both
Mary Rose's mothers?
Are we not one?

I Miss My Baby

I wake up the day after labor without you,
    Mary Rose.

                I miss my baby.

Your milk fills me
    the day after your burial.

                I miss my baby.

One month goes by, then two.

                I miss my baby.

I make an excavator costume for my boy.
    Thanksgiving, Christmas cards, cookies and presents.
It's time to order the headstone, Tim says.

                I miss my baby.

Almost six months.
    First time in Outer Banks, Kitty Hawk, Manteo.

                I miss my baby.

Krissy births a healthy baby, then Melania, Mikey, now Nick, Stephen.
    Two newborns baptized in church.

                I miss my baby.

The priest comes to bless the house.
    Your brother will turn three.
        La linea negra fades. . . .

                I miss my baby.

Should we try again?
    You'll be 43 and I'll be 49.

                I miss my baby.

Do willows really weep?

                I miss my baby.

Meditation on Mother's Words

1.

I am pregnant – no
I was pregnant
and the baby would die.

Mother asked
What if you get pregnant again
and the next baby has Down syndrome?

At the rest stop coming down
from the mountains a baby boy
        with Down syndrome
eating more easily than my son –
his father smiles.

2.

Mongoloid. Mongoloid.

The TV is on. I am a girl. My mother
is watching a documentary on Down syndrome.

masticate

My daughter had trisomy 18.
Down syndrome is trisomy 21.

mobilize

The man at the creek in Golden, Colorado
also with Down syndrome looks into my eyes.
        Hi, I'm Tim, he says.

My husband Tim is in the water with our son.

melody

Mother, after Mary Rose
I had an early miscarriage

meander

3.

I remember every disabled child
and adult I have met since
the ultrasound in March 2014.

                    monsoon

My heart center said *trisomy, trisomy*
and I knew before the phone call
confirming . . .

                    Master!

The 3-yr old girl at the zoo,
the babies born still
or living for hours or days
and Grace who lived for six weeks.

                    mercurius

Our babies in coffins

                    mother's milk

You had a choice, you could have aborted

                    melancholy

4.

I am pregnant again and afraid –
no – not afraid.

                    manifest

The child is the child with its perfect DNA

                    mysticism

I am pregnant for the fourth time

                    mellifluous

baby conceived on the full moon super moon
    blood moon   total lunar eclipse

        miracles not Mongoloid

Are we morons or mystics?

        mercy   mercy

Oh Mother, another

        miscarriage.

Part IV

The Art of Grieving

I honor myself, my uterus, my wombspace –
my baby's precious and sacred home.

Mary Burgess with Shiloh Sophia McCloud

The Art of Grieving

AS A TRAINED POETRY THERAPIST and writer, I know the therapeutic value of writing through grief and life's challenges. I kept a journal from the time of Mary Rose's diagnosis, and continue writing to this day. It is important to discuss the healing benefits of working through grief by making art, whether that art is a poem, essay, painting or a dance. I worked through my initial grief by creating poems and artwork. This valuable experience could benefit many mourning parents.

Most of us have heard of art therapy, but there are many other therapies such as poetry therapy, drama therapy and dance/movement therapy. These therapeutic techniques help us cope with the emotional turmoil of our grief. We are not very grounded in our bodies in our hyper-electronic, busy lifestyles. We flit around from task to task staying busy, doing, doing, pushing through exhaustion. We do not know how to *be*. We know how to *do*. In order to be, we need to have some sense of the body. To understand the body, we also have to recognize the mind and the way our brain works, as well as the soul which seeks nourishment.

When I came across the grief workbook co-created by Mary Burgess and Shiloh Sophia McCloud called *Mending Invisible Wings: Healing From the Loss of Your Baby* (*MIW*), it became an important part of my initial grief processing during the postpartum period. Burgess is a doula whose first birth as a doula ended in the baby's death. McCloud is an artist who worked through the grief of her own miscarriage. Her drawings appear throughout *MIW*. Burgess and McCloud put together this book in order to create a way for others to cope with miscarriage and infant loss. We in America feel that we are due, or somehow can earn, a healthy living newborn by taking vitamins, eating right and exercising. The reality is that women sometimes miscarry and that babies sometimes die. I am grateful that these instances are not the majority of our pregnancies, but how do those of us who have experienced infant death and miscarriage process our own fears and grief in a culture that turns away from our reality?

MIW is beautiful from the cover image to the thick, blank pages inviting us to become artists and writers in our grief. The exercises include writing and drawing prompts, rituals, meditation, affirmation, breathing exercises and guided visualizations. We are taken back to the body that we want to escape: the body that conceived the child, the womb that housed and nourished her, the passageway through which she emerged. You may color McCloud's drawings, read about infant death or write and create as deeply as you desire. Let's remember that we are not just grieving people whose children have died. We are also traumatized people who have received terrible news during pregnancy or right after birth, and lived through a birth that did not yield the outcomes that we desired. We let go of a dream and a child. Our trauma is profound and there is no way of going around it. In order to heal, we must sit in the muck and feel the chaotic refrains of guilt, anger, sadness, grief, loneliness, resentment and whatever else comes up so that we can transmute these feelings into Light.

In the letter to the reader Burgess and McCloud write,

> Please think of this journal as your unbiased, non-judgmental pregnancy and birth loss witness – a living, inviting entity that listens fully as you write and draw and create your story. . . . It is essential for you, the mother, to love your body, accept and incorporate your experiences, and to grieve – fully, gently – so that you may heal wholly. Certainly, this does not mean that in doing so, you will forget your Spirit Child or abandon those memories; in fact, it is just the opposite (17).

We are reminded by the co-creators that we need to be gentle with ourselves as we honor our bodies that have been through so much. I worked through the first half of the book in the fall after my baby died in August.

I spent many hours in therapy as I wrote and processed my emotions and trauma surrounding my pregnancy with Mary Rose in *MIW*. The workbook is beneficial, but might require additional support that can be found in infant loss support groups, appointments with chaplains, priests, pastors, rabbis, as well as good, compassionate therapists. Wonderful counsel is also available from nuns and monks in various monastic traditions. It is helpful to understand how the brain processes trauma with a professional in the field. Eye Movement Desensitization and Reprocessing (EMDR) can heal trauma, and some therapists offer this treatment. Information on Tapping, also known as Emotional Freedom Technique, another trauma healing modality, is available online.

One of the first prompts in the workbook begins *Today, I feel . . .* (29). I respond,

> Today, I feel . . .
> shattered, broken, exhausted
> filled with pain, sadness, grief
> droopy, weepy, lonely for my baby
> sad my son is without a living sibling
> sad I'm 42, sad I held my baby dead
> shattered, all innocence lost, holy, sacred path.

Then I start to draw myself as a tree. My body is the golden bark. My hands are folded over what would be my uterus, and my heart is bright and red and shattered. There is no smile on my face. I am grounded in the earth with leaves growing behind my head. I do a few of these tree images. In the final one I merge with the tree, and all that is left of my human form is my heart weeping and watering my roots. *I water my / roots with / tears from / my broken heart, / open heart*, I write on one side. *Oh uterus, / breasts / empty and forlorn*, I write on the other side of the tree. *Where is my baby?* is at the base of the tree, and underneath *Mary Rose / becomes dust. / My work becomes dust. / Hard work. / Holy work.*

Another section in *MIW* is called "A Letter to Me . . . A Letter to My Child" (35). I start by writing a letter to myself:

> Woman, why do you weep? Your daughter is in the safest place, completely healed. A place with no illness or despair, no pain or sadness. No grief. Walk tall. Be proud that you carried this AWE-some soul, this spiritual genius and protec-tress of all that is sacred and holy. Your body, your womb, brought her to the earth once again to bless, to carry, to nurture and hold space for so many, even as your words heal on many planes. This is your sacred passageway and initiation to your Life's work: more + more + more LOVE. Amen.

I write a letter to Mary Rose:

> Mary Rose, I wish I could have sheltered your body from my raging, wracking grief. Was my body a storm tossing you about or was my womb a sanctuary of holy love for the daughter I always wanted and loved, the one who gives love so freely, who honors all from the angelic realms, flying to us and protecting us al-ways until we step through the portal – that holy threshold into the LIGHT?

Underneath I draw an angel with a heart in her center and light radiating all around her. I had been holding intense guilt that I cried and worried during my pregnancy. If Mary Rose's time on earth was almost completely in my womb, then what kind of life did I give her?

In the section "Birth: Baby's Perspective – A Sensual Journey" (52–54), I write from Mary Rose's perspective:

> My birth, like my life, was short, sweet, filled with Love.
> The hands that touched me were gentle and loving and tired
> from their earth living, their heartaches and heartbreaks.
> The Light was gentle, the words and sounds soothing.
> Sadness was not the primary emotion, though your heart,
> Mother, was heavy with weeping and grieving for a reunion
> we couldn't yet have, but will have again. My blankets were soft
> the caresses were gentle, Love rained on my soul that day,
> And my brother's Love, forever is with me.
> There is no separation
> > Only United Unity
> We know the truth

> About the Soul
> About Life.
> Let others quibble about this or that.
> We walk together in union and love.
> Fulfilling our Mission and Purpose.
> The Angelic realms proclaim it.
> We are One
> We are Love
> Your gentle kisses, Mother,
> Sustain me until we meet soul to soul
> Spirit to Spirit to Spirit.
> Aho, Selah. Om.

I draw an angel from an image I had in a meditation at the end of the pregnancy. I saw myself holding a small baby, and out of her body a huge surge of energy and light bursts forth and shoots out in every direction. When I read *MIW,* I spent some quiet time reflecting on the pregnancy, and I remembered that image and wanted to capture it. I drew and painted an angel of light that emerges from the infant body. This image is now the cover of this book.

One blank journal page has the following words:

> You were
>
> barely alive and
>
> you slipped away quietly,
>
> my sweet, quiet, little girl.

Another day I write:

> How did
> this
> happen?
> Sad
> empty
> sagging
> body.

I draw myself naked with sagging breasts and tears dripping out of my body and eyes.

There is something about the blank, thick pages in this workbook that gave me permission to open up and start processing in the physical world of art and words. In the picture I drew of the birth scene, another prompt in the workbook, I am standing in the pool surrounded by the ones who were there at the moment of birth. The artwork is crude and the characters speak in bubbles. At the top: *Day of Mary Rose, An Hour of Mary Rose,* and at the bottom: *An Annunciation, A Nativity, A Falling Asleep, A Resurrection,* four of the major Feasts of the Orthodox Church. My therapist had discussed Mary Rose as my annunciation, but I didn't understand. She explained that I accepted the child as she was. *Be it unto me according to Thy word, Oh Lord.* Waiting for a baby to be born is a Nativity. We wait and prepare to make space in our homes for the newborn. The Feast of the Dormition of the *Theotokos* or God-Bearer is on August 15. It is said that Mother Mary was taken up by Christ after she died, like the prophet Elijah. Finally, the Resurrection comes after death. St. John Chrysostom's words *O Death where is thy sting?* (47) are read each year during the Paschal service, and when I was in a spiritual frame of mind, I knew that Mary Rose was a gift and a life-changing experience. The problem was my hurting, leaking body and hormones looking for the baby. We cannot walk this life only in spirit. By giving us our bodies, God has called us to do both. We must honor our bodies by feeding and emptying and resting them just as we must do the same for our souls.

In the picture I am cheered on by midwives and doula. Midwife Grace's words, *Let her do her work,* still resonate with me. The women gather around mother and child while my husband looks straight ahead. *I'll deal with it when I get there,* he says. And he did. He tenderly held our daughter in his big hands and showed her love during her brief life. My two-year-old says, *Mary Rose, my sister.* Sindy takes pictures with her camera. My mother is there witnessing Mary Rose's life-changing birth. The colors are yellow and gold because that is how I remember the experience. That golden light shielded her from the outside world in a holy scene of birth. We were safe. We were loved. We were present for whatever life had to offer us in those moments: a sweet babe, a falling asleep, a resurrection.

In the picture I stand in the blood and meconium of birth straddling life and death in one life-changing moment, surrounded by others with their own words and thoughts. This gives me a bigger view of the reality of Mary Rose's birth. Her life was never just about me. She is my daughter, but she is also someone's sister, someone's granddaughter. She came for many. The blank page and the pencil in my fingers on the warm autumn days following Mary Rose's birth gave me a way to draw my grief out instead of keeping it inside.

Following the birth scene artwork, I draw a labyrinth with me standing toward the outer periphery, stepping in, away from the outside world to do my work as Mary Rose's mother. The path is strewn with roses and is not straight. I did not walk from her conception to birth as I had in my previous pregnancy. Instead I had to stay flexible and present in each moment as things changed. Sometimes I went this way and sometimes that way. The labyrinth is a place where people walk peacefully, where they can see the next step. We know what is at the center, even though it will take time to get there. I slow down and take small steps, holding onto my daughter who is both one with me and the center of the meandering path. My labyrinth's center is my heart; it is also Mary Rose. The title of this book and my blog came from this exercise. *Walking the Labyrinth of My Heart.* Although I am surrounded by people in Mary Rose's birth scene, here I stand alone. This is one of the dualities of human existence. As much as we need community and support, we also walk our path alone with Creator. No one could birth Mary Rose but me, just as our own birth and death are solitary steps in the wheel of life. I had a community during my pregnancy, but I also felt alone carrying my baby, alone those long nighttime hours, alone feeling her tiny movements.

In my fear and anxiety about Mary Rose's condition, I was able to muster the strength to create a safe and quiet birth for her. I took care of her in life and in death. The Dianna in the labyrinth picture is resolved and anxious. I wish I knew then that babies who live with trisomy 18 do not usually suffer. I wish I had not been afraid. But I walked my path, my labyrinth, to the center of my heart with as much dignity and grace as my limping body could gather. I have no regrets except my worry. I write now to you, Dear Reader, as you walk your own labyrinth. Your baby will do what your baby is coming to do. God is merciful. As Jane Kenyon says in her poem "Let Evening Come,"

> Let it come, as it will, and don't
> be afraid. God does not leave us
> comfortless, so let evening come (69).

MIW's exercises gave me different lenses with which to view my experience with Mary Rose. Evening came and I was okay. I didn't think that I could survive my pregnancy, but I did. I recommend the process of these exercises, but you don't have to buy the book and go through it step by step. You can also create your own exercises to remember and process your experience.

Exercises and Tools to Heal Grief

WRITING, DRAWING AND PAINTING can be done in one place like a journal or a canvas. Many of my suggestions are interchangeable and can be used to create mixed-media works. I like collage, writing, drawing and painting. You do not need any experience to do this. No one will see your work unless you choose to share it. My friend Terry broke dishes and made mosaics after her second daughter, Holly, died of cystic fibrosis. I wrote and drew and painted and made things. It doesn't matter what we create specifically. It is the process that allows us to grieve and to heal, but first we need tools to do so. Some of this work will bring up torrential tears. Sometimes we have to stop and seek help through therapy or group support. It is nearly impossible to come to an understanding and acceptance of infant death by ourselves.

In creating poems and artwork, we are taking some of our grief out of our shattered hearts and putting it into something: a blank page, a canvas, a wooden box. As we process our buried emotions and trauma, we create art from our shock and sadness. There is research that shows the benefits of creative arts therapies. Writing or drawing will not take away your sadness completely, but it will lighten your load as you undergo a catharsis or cleansing. It is beautiful work – even when it is dark and raw and unpolished. Sometimes the poem or drawing or dance can be a gift to your own self, a sacred gift that does not need to be shared with anyone. Following are a few suggestions to process grief, though there are many other modalities out there to support individuals. (Knitting, coloring and cooking come to mind.)

Journal Writing: Get a blank notebook or journal. I like books with no lines so that I can sketch and write. You can decorate the cover of the book with stickers, ribbons, buttons, magazine photos or your own pictures. Record your feelings of grief periodically or daily. I often wrote a few lines, or drew an angel with a heart in her center. Sometimes I could only write *I miss you, Mary Rose*. Recording our feelings and thoughts through the pregnancy and the time after birth and death is helpful on many levels. It memorializes our loved ones as we create a work of beauty about them. However raw the drawing or poem, it has value.

Poetry or Creative Nonfiction: Take a poem that you love and find a line that resonates with you. You can use Jane Kenyon's poem "Let Evening Come" or Marie Howe's poem "What the Living Do." Take one line from the model poem as a prompt to write your own poem. For the two poems mentioned above, I like to start with the title of Kenyon's poem "Let Evening Come" as a title of my poem. From the title, I write images and start the poetic process. For Howe's poem, the line "I am living. I remember you" makes a good starting point. Do not think; just let the pencil or pen do the work of getting some of the grief from your heart onto the page.

Another way to write through grief is to start a longer nonfiction essay by writing separate sections. Brenda Miller's essays are good examples. If you want to learn more about the illness that took your baby's life, then you might want to do some research and write some of what you find in a section or two. You can write about the moment of diagnosis in one section, or the shock of the death in another. Write about the funeral or memorial service, or how there was none. Create a ritual through your writing, talk about people's reactions to your experience, etc. You can build a much longer work through fragments and reflections.

Painting: Get a blank sketchbook with thicker paper so that you can use watercolors, if you choose. Close your eyes and take a few deep breaths. Think about your baby and your pregnancy. Think about your womb and your breasts. What images come up? Draw them. Paint them. Write about them. Create a mixed-media work and dialogue with your body and your broken heart.

Collage: I made a collage of the sympathy cards that I received on a memory box for my daughter's few belongings. However, a collage can be a poster, a canvas, a journal. I cut up cards, used color copies of artwork of Mother Mary, cloth butterflies and flowers, stickers and acrylic paint.

Yoga and Meditation Music: The yoga stretches accompanied by meditation music such as Wah!'s music allow the breath to change the moment. I start out tight on my yoga mat with pain coursing through my hips and legs, and, slowly with the breath and with the positions, I shift my energy and my physical body. A yoga practice can be very helpful in the intensity of grief. Crying on the mat is just fine as we continue to move forward one pose at a time peacefully or by processing our anger and rage.

Dance and Movement: Belly dancing or other movement through classes offered in your community can be very beneficial. Getting back into the body after the trauma of miscarriage or infant death and postpartum hormones is a good way to heal the trauma. I do a combination of yoga, belly dance, walking meditation and walking by a lake weekly. Doing this alone or with other women can be helpful in moving forward and taking your child's spirit with you into the rest of your life. The repetition of the movement, the moments away from the daily routine and the actual physical work help us to reset our thought process.

Drumming: The rhythm of a drumbeat can be a very soothing meditation that can lead to healing. In many cultures the drum is used to transcend the reality of this realm and help the suffering person work toward healing. The drumbeat sounds like a heartbeat and connects us to each other, Earth and our ancestors. Shamanic healing includes drumming, and Sandra Ingerman has a few CDs and meditations that are helpful to walk through grief into a place of peace.

Chanting and Praying: Qigong and yoga chants have been very helpful for me to process some of the intense grief and weeping into new energy. The sounds of the Qigong or Sanskrit mantra carry higher vibrations, as does the Orthodox prayer *Lord Jesus have mercy on me* repeated over and over. I pray *Hail Mary* again and again. The repetition is helpful in shifting from extreme grief into a space of quiet meditation or contemplation.

Garden: Create a memorial garden for your loved one. I have a tiny fairy sculpture in a container with a small fairy rosebush. You don't need a lot of space or an elaborate garden to honor the life of your child.

Part V

Cubby LaHood

We can do no great things,
only small things with great love.

Mother Teresa

THE ROSA MYSTICA

WHEN I THINK ABOUT my pregnancy journey with Mary Rose, I cannot unstitch the experience from certain relationships that came to be because of my daughter. My daughter brought me Grace and Elizabeth, Sindy, Leslie and Cubby. When I wrote to Nancy Mayer-Whittington thanking her for her book, I knew that she had co-founded Isaiah's Promise with Cubby LaHood. She writes about this toward the end of her book *For the Love of Angela*. When Cubby responded to my email to Nancy, I was surprised. She began a beautiful relationship of mentorship and sweet gifts for Mary Rose. There are people who supported me, lifted me up from the heaviness of my grief and shock. I am so blessed to have an amazing therapist, a holy homeopath, and friends and close relatives who love me. Cubby stands out because she was a stranger. She leapt into my life and heart without the boundaries that separate most humans from each other.

My relationship with Cubby was intense. She spoke from her heart and gave me her opinions when she did not agree with me. Some of her most touching correspondence is shared here with the permission of her husband, Dan, and daughter, Mary Frances. Unless otherwise noted, all of her words come from her emails to me. We spoke only once on the phone, quickly, to exchange phone numbers for texting when she was in the hospital undergoing treatment for stage 4 cancer.

Cubby never told me that she had cancer when I was pregnant. She didn't want to give her moms anything else to think about. We continued to correspond after Mary Rose died, and she told me about her own struggles in the fall of 2014. Cubby continued to give when others could not. She replied to one of my texts a week before she died, after a stroke and a fall. *Does she need support? Books? Welcome packet?* referring to a mother with a baby death.

Congratulations on doing the most important thing in your life, she writes to me on August 9, 2014. It was the day of my newborn's funeral. This one sentence is a good example of Cubby's faith and strength. She supported my family, especially my daughter, with unwavering love. Following is her first correspondence:

May 24, 2014

Please shoot me an email!! It would be good to get you turned around about the LIFE of your daughter now!! While she is here! :) We have a great prayer partner list and folks pray every day for our families. . . . You really will be OK with some support around you – you are not the only mama doing this – although it can CERTAINLY feel that way – we ARE a minority. I would LOVE to hear from you!! In Friendship, Cubby

In a few days I had five packages from Isaiah's Promise with books and gifts for my unborn baby. I was so touched. I didn't know that this would continue, as Isaiah's Promise volunteers remembered Mary Rose after she died and on what would have been her first birthday.

Cubby wrote many words that lifted me up and resonated with me. Her son, Francis Edward, died after birth of a kidney disorder. She was a mother who carried a baby with a fatal diagnosis with unwavering love. She was a woman who buried her newborn baby. She was also a woman who kept her son alive in her family, who considered him an intercessor. As a mentor, Cubby offered me guidance based on her own experiences. She dedicated decades of her life in service to parents and their dying babies through Isaiah's Promise. Cubby and her husband also ran a day-care center, St. Joseph's House, for the severely disabled. Many people offer the words, *I know what you're going through*, with no such knowledge, but Cubby did know. She had walked through the difficulties and knew how we felt. Her words still reverberate with love and kindness.

May 25, 2014

Do not be afraid of her or of the birth. Try to embrace the fact that she has worked hard all this time to stay with you – most babies with issues are miscarried – so Mary Rose is a GIFT – even if she passes – she is a GIFT because you have been given the opportunity by GOD to love her unconditionally – with all your heart. Our babies are NOT "throw away babies" as our society says – they are just maybe too broken for this world. You will have a saint in Heaven to pray to.

I write to Cubby about how hard it is to be in my pregnant body during the pregnancy. I confide in her that instead of counting forward to 40 weeks of pregnancy, I start to count backwards. *Eight weeks left,* I write. I speak of my anxiety for my sensitive son. She always writes back answering each of my concerns and adds some of her own. She does not like the idea of a home birth and worries about Mary Rose's and my safety. She speaks to midwife Grace a few times. They work together to give us some memories such as Christmas ornaments we decorate with Mary Rose's footprints and my son's handprints. Cubby's faith comes forth always, but also her devotion to serving others and her love for all the babies in the world who are challenged.

May 26, 2014

Yes, the suffering is what we all worry about so much. Its like a catch 22, we want them here with us, but we also want God to take them. You must not feel guilty, you have carried her because you love her – in life we all suffer in some way, even a healthy child suffers along the way. It is just that Mary Rose will have all the joy, love, and suffering, in a short period of life. . . . With all the babies I have helped deliver – I have not seen suffering. It has always been very, very peaceful, like falling asleep. Even with Francis, it was slow and peaceful and I was not afraid. We held him always. You won't need any equipment because you will not be putting her down!!

All of the parents that we have worked with made their own decision about carrying to term and NONE have regretted it. People/society are very uncomfortable with carrying to term – surround yourself with people who understand and care about you, your family and Mary Rose.

Mary Rose deserves dignity . . . she will always live in your heart. She will give you strength.

May 31, 2014

Oh My Friend – I know how hard it is. . . . I would stare out the window at our swing set and weep, knowing my son would never play there. . . . However, the closer I got to delivery, the more I became calm because I wanted to MEET him after all those months. . . . I wanted to hold him and love him even if that was all we could do. . . . I was HIS mother and I would cherish him every second. All of my fear and doubts would ebb and flow, but on delivery day I was only ready for love. I really prayed hard for strength. God gave me this baby son – if only for a few minutes. And I was going to love him – I had no idea that I was to be a witness to HIM for all those stupid people who ignored or pretended my pregnancy did not exist. . . . So I stayed close to the people who understood. . . . The stupid people will find their way – it's because they are really afraid and could never imagine being such a beautiful and brave mom as you are – try to put that stuff aside – it's not worth your energy. You KNOW there are people who love you and Mary Rose – I have you ALL on my prayer list that goes out to approximately 100 people on Isaiah's Promise prayer list. . . .

Try bringing some LIGHT into the dark by thanking God for this opportunity for unconditional love. You were chosen as her mother – it is YOU that GOD gave this treasure to!! Handpicked – because he knew you would love with all of your heart. It is not a punishment – it is a gift – an opportunity to widen your heart to all of your family. To show that you love no matter what – after all – should another child become sick – say a child of one of your friends who does not understand?? Would they leave them alone? Of course not. They would TAKE CARE of them!!! . . .

June 18, 2014

YOU are stronger than YOU think – right now it is all the unknowns that make life so tedious – after birth, things will fall into place – even though you sense that Mary Rose's time will be short – you must begin to look forward to meeting her – whatever the outcome. Love and letting go will be a part of it – but nothing is more important than love. . . .

In the meantime – we will keep praying for you, especially for strength – and remember LOOK forward to meeting her – God has given you a great gift.

June 24, 2014

When/if she dies – you will understand that this is what you must do. . . . It's all a part of caring for her in a proper and dignified way. You must show your son that one can still love even when the person is gone, you must show him that you are a strong mama who chose to give life. . . .

You will be OK . . . because you must be OK for your son – and to be a witness to life – in your quiet moments and probably the funeral – you will fall apart because you have lost something irreplaceable – but you WILL also always have her . . . but not in your arms – in your heart. We DO survive burying our children . . . and we all receive many graces from our babies – they are our treasures always. Keep in touch! xxoo

When I tell Cubby that my friend, Dr. Daniela Ragusa, is using Isaiah's Promise's website and Mary Rose's story as a text in her composition class at Capital Community College in Hartford, Connecticut, she offers to send books to Daniela and then replies, *See what Mary Rose has done!!!??? A college class! All that from a very wise babe!!*

On February 8, 2015, I send Cubby an email. *Today it is six months.* She responds,

Your six month anniversary – a hard one. I used to count by Fridays as that is the day he was born – now of course I count by years – and many beautiful gifts have come through the years when I least expected. This will be you too. . . . Be patient, which is hard to do! xx Keep an open heart. Beautiful daughter.

Francis and Mary Rose were both born on a Friday. They both died on a Friday. Again and again Cubby talks about doing small things with great love. I think of Mary Rose's few belongings, many of them gifts from volunteers at Isaiah's Promise. After Mary Rose died, the gifts continued. A picture book about death for my son. A pink stocking with my daughter's name for Christmas. Small pink booties with her name on the one-year anniversary of her death. All small things that add up to a lot of love.

Cubby and I texted and emailed about Mother Gavrielia, the Greek Orthodox nun, St. Therese, the Little Flower, St. Anthimos of Chios, a healer. I told Cubby that I was praying for him to heal her. She wanted to be at the college graduation of her daughter, Mary Frances, and made it. She asked me to pray that she lives until 2016 to be at her youngest son's high school graduation. Cubby died on September 21, 2015, but she said she was supposed to die years ago. They sent her home on hospice the year before, but she found an NIH study that gave her a few more months. We speak of courage in our culture in a flip way. Cubby wasn't courageous or strong, she was fierce and loving, devout and a bit of a spitfire.

I was able to share the Isaiah's Promise mission with Sister Evelyn of Mount St. Mary's Abbey before Cubby died. Cubby sent some books and materials to Sister Evelyn and they began to correspond. Sister Evelyn admired Cubby's determination even in the face of death to serve her mothers, to continue her work here on earth. Even close to the very end of her life she continued to give: stories, encouragement, books, love. How blessed I am to be one of her last mothers she mentored through Isaiah's Promise.

I wouldn't hear from Cubby for several days and I would think, *She must have died.* Then I would get a message from her again. One time in June she wrote that she had died.

> Priest came to give me last rites and I woke up!! Haha guess I was not ready – I did give the MAN upstairs a high five though. I am home now resting – Gonna have a beer!!

She had that human resilience that poets write about again and again. Who was this woman? I never met her in person, yet she changed my life.

Cubby died between my two miscarriages. She knew of the first one. She continued to encourage me to trust God. *I was 43 with my youngest*, she writes. After my second miscarriage in October, I cried wishing for a text from Cubby. Is there a vocation of Encourager? That is what she was and still is. Her words live on, and her life continues to reach out far and wide as her influence grows even in death, just as it is with our children.

When I was still pregnant with Mary Rose, Cubby told me about the Rosa Mystica. It was June and Cubby was sick, but I did not know this yet. *I am taking care of her*, she told me. I googled Rosa Mystica and learned of more miracles of Our Lady. I learned that the rose is her flower. *Mary Rose.* I didn't know the significance of the name that entered my heart when I was pregnant. I believe that Cubby had the statue in her home, that there was to be a prayer service that night. *I will pray for you and Mary Rose*, she told me.

And she still does.

Epilogue

AFTER MY SECOND MISCARRIAGE in October, my therapist suggested that I read Clarissa Pinkola Estés' book *The Faithful Gardener*. In her book Dr. Estés tells a story within a story. "Like *Matryoshka* dolls," she writes, "they fit one inside the other" (3). And like nesting dolls, our own birth stories, our children, our pregnancies, miscarriages, infertility challenges fit one inside the other. Mary Rose is now connected to my first midwife, Vicki, and her nephew, John Gilbert, and my former officemate, Isabel, and her niece, Grace Miriam, as well as many others. We tell one story, and it leads to another story of a baby who died of trisomy 18 or anencephaly or SIDS.

At some point after pregnancy the womb is empty, a fallow field in our own birthing journey. Sometimes the womb is seeded again, sometimes not in the way that we desire. What is it like for a womb after a child has died in it or right after birth? What is it like for the body that is ready to nourish with milk and embraces, when there is no living child to feed and hold? An empty womb is a relief when the baby breathes and eats and cries in her mother's arms. Not so for the rest of us who bear infant death.

In *The Faithful Gardener* Dr. Estés tells the story of immigrants from Europe escaping World War II: the camps, the hunger, the utter senselessness of injustice. These refugees are broken and do not say much about their past, but they tell stories. After roads were built through some of the farmland her family worked, Dr. Estés' uncle appeared to go mad when they abused more land than was needed for the highway. He gathered shovels and dug a trench with the help of his neighbors. Dr. Estés writes,

> There in the field, in the completely windless night, he carefully poured the fuel all along the field on two sides and down the middle. . . . The entire field erupted in a blaze so great that it drew people . . . watching the field burn and burn. . . .
>
> "So you see," Uncle said, "this burning and blackening of the soil here? Soon much will come of it, so much that you will not believe it" (34–35).

Dr. Estés is a little girl here, and when she asks her uncle what he will seed in the field, he replies that he will seed nothing. Uncle says,

> ". . . you leave the ground fallow. What does that mean? It means you leave it turned, but unsown. It means you send it through fire in order to prepare it for its new life. . . fire comes. Though we are afraid, it comes anyway, sometimes by accident, sometimes on purpose, sometimes for reasons no one can understand – reasons that are God's business alone.
>
> But the fire can also turn everything to a new direction, a new and different life, one that has its own strengths and ways to shape the world" (37–38).

In time a forest grew. It took years, as it often does, but seedlings of trees and many plants sprouted. Dr. Estés ends her book after a few more stories by telling us that she burned her own field in Boulder, Colorado, on a windless day, then cried and christened it for some time to honor her ancestors. By the third year she has two maples four feet tall and many other seedlings and small trees. Even wild onions and herbs seed themselves on the land. Butterflies, crickets and other living creatures follow (71-72). She writes,

> I know that those who are in some ways and for some time shorn of belief in life itself – that they ultimately are the ones who will come to know best that Eden lies underneath an empty field, that the new seed goes first to the empty and open places – even when the open place is a grieving heart, a tortured mind, or a devastated spirit...what has seemed dead is dead no longer, what has seemed lost, is no longer lost, that which some have claimed impossible, is made clearly possible, and what ground is fallow is only resting – resting and waiting for the blessed seed to arrive on the wind with all Godspeed.
>
> And it will (74–75).

I wept as I read the book the first time, and then read it again, marking many passages. This field, or no, the heart, and the womb, that is broken and cleared and burned is what I have been writing about and living since my daughter's diagnosis – no, since my first husband's psychotic breakdown, since Jeanette took her young life, since my Matina suffered from meningioma, since the distance from my family in Greece hurts me inside. . . . We have all been broken and bereft, but the death of an infant, the end of a pregnancy with a stillborn or miscarriage is so profoundly painful that now I understand it is as if my very soul were burned to the ground. I weep. I cry out. I search and search for my daughter as Demeter did, but she is not in physical form. She is no longer on my earth.

I wait. I wait for seeds to blow into my heart and body once again, but also into my womb, into my family and my writing career. This waiting and time is what we don't have in our post-9/11 world. We ask, *How long will this take?* speaking of grief. We rush through grief and our days. We are here on earth surrounded by the love of the ancestors, blessed beyond measure, but missing a part of our life on earth. Rushing does not take the grief away. I will not rush through my journey processing my daughter's pregnancy and death. I wait. I was 42. I am 43. I wait.

When my daughter first died, I was speaking to Aniela, my homeopath and friend, about my son. She told me to watch my language so as not to blame God for Mary Rose's death. She told me to tell my son that God is the kind gardener who plants our souls in the garden where we thrive best. I used this metaphor a few times. *Mary Rose is in the heavenly garden,* I repeat to him. He always answers, *I want to go to heaven. I want to be with my sister, Mary Rose.* Following is the Bahá'í prayer that illustrates this metaphor of God as the Gardener from Selections of 'Abdu'l-Bahá. It begins by specifically addressing the death of someone young:

> ... The death of that beloved youth and his separation from you have caused the utmost sorrow and grief; for he winged his flight in the flower of his age and the bloom of his youth to the heavenly nest. ...
>
> The inscrutable divine wisdom underlieth such heart-rending occurrences. It is as if a kind gardener transferreth a fresh and tender shrub from a confined place to a wide open area. This transfer is not the cause of the withering, the lessening or the destruction of that shrub; nay, on the contrary, it maketh it to grow and thrive, acquire freshness and delicacy, become green and bear fruit. This hidden secret is well known to the gardener, but those souls who are unaware of this bounty suppose that the gardener, in his anger and wrath, hath uprooted the shrub. Yet to those who are aware, this concealed fact is manifest, and this predestined decree is considered a bounty. ...

As a mother of a child who has died, I choose to believe in resurrection and transfiguration and heavenly gardens. I was powerless in the face of trisomy 18 to do anything other than love my daughter. I knew that I could not change her outcomes, nor change her life span. But I was her advocate for the home birth and the quiet blessing of preparing her body for burial. Now I am an advocate for myself: for my life after her death, which includes raising my son with my beloved husband, healing my body and believing in a future that is not constrained by sadness alone. Mary Rose is not my first loss. She is one of many, but she was flesh of my flesh. The space where she is no longer, is in my body. Each day I make a choice to smile, to notice a bird searching for worms, to pay attention to the wind and the chimes and the shadows and the branches' silhouette during twilight. Only through the lens of love can I make sense of my daughter's life.

To live with infant death is to live. We get dressed (most days), step outside, cook, gather our loved ones to us. Not a day goes by when I do not think of Mary Rose. Not an hour. ... My heart has been burned of all that was. Now I wait and know that whatever comes is meant to live and grow here. I offer my cleared heart to the life that always returns, to the seeds and bugs and life that come again.

dear mother who is bereaved

walk the winding path
follow the light up
heart light
seed light
hands on unborn baby light

you too: light
transfigured on the mount

labor comes: grief can be
sorrow
transformed

twilight   soon mourning
look: sunlight through the trees

...in the heavenly garden

Mary Rose

Siddhartha Izarra

Jacob Alexander

Grace Miriam

David Isaac

Angela Marie

Emily Southworth

Madeleine

Rosemary

Cubby

Grace Mary

John Gilbert

Francis Edward

Nora Ann

Alexia Christine

Harrison Cuffley

Zinnia Wild Grace

Bryson James

Ryder Chance

Angelica Marie

Kira Marie

Kira Lee

Isaac Quinn

and all our babies gone too soon

Works Cited

'Abdu'l-Bahá. "Selections from the Writings of 'Abdu'l-Bahá." Bahá'í International Community Bahá'í Reference Library. Bahá'í World Center, 1982. Web. 25 Jan. 2016.

Barnes, Ann M., and John C. Carey. *Care of the Infant and Child with Trisomy 18 or Trisomy 13: A Care Book for Families*. 3rd ed. Omaha, NE: Munroe-Meyer Institute for Genetics and Rehabilitation, University of Nebraska Medical Center, 2014. Web.

Bratton, Marietta W., ed. *I Will Bear This Scar: Poems of Childless Women*. New York, NY: iUniverse, Inc., 2005. Print.

Brooks, Arthur. "Choose to Be Grateful. It Will Make You Happier." Op. Ed. *New York Times*, 21 Nov. 2015. Web. 23 Nov. 2015.

Burgess, Mary, with Shiloh Sophia McCloud. *Mending Invisible Wings: Healing from the Loss of Your Baby*. Healdsburg, CA: Palm of Her Hand, 2009. Print.

Estés, Clarissa Pinkola. *The Faithful Gardener: A Wise Tale about That Which Can Never Die*. San Francisco, CA: HarperCollins, 1995. Print.

——. *Women Who Run with the Wolves: Myths and Stories of the Wild Woman Archetype*. New York, NY: Ballantine Books, 1992. Print.

Glenn, Amy Wright. *Birth, Breath, and Death: Meditations on Motherhood, Chaplaincy, and Life as a Doula*. North Charleston, SC: CreateSpace Independent Publishing Platform, 2013. Print.

Greenberg, Arielle, and Rachel Zucker. *Home/Birth: A Poemic*. 1913 Press. 2011. Print.

Harman, Patricia. *The Midwife of Hope River*. New York, NY: William Morrow, 2012. Print.

Harper, Elizabeth. *Wishing: How to Fulfill Your Heart's Desires*. New York, NY: Atria Books, 2008. Print.

The Holy Bible, King James Version. Cambridge edition, 1769; *King James Bible Online*, 2016. Web. 31 Jan. 2016.

Howe, Marie. *What the Living Do*. New York, NY: W.W. Norton & Company, 1998. Print.

Jones-Brady, Terry. *A Mosaic Heart: Reshaping the Shards of a Shattered Life*. Charlottesville, VA: Quartet Books, 2011. Print.

Katie, Byron. *Loving What Is*. New York, NY: Harmony Books, 2002. Print.

Kenyon, Jane. *Let Evening Come*. Saint Paul, MN: Graywolf Press, 1990. Print.

Kenyon, Mary Potter. *Refined by Fire: A Journey of Grief and Grace.* Sanger, CA: Familius, 2014.

Kunitz, Stanley. *Passing Through: The Later Poems New and Selected.* New York, NY: W.W. Norton & Company, 1995. Print.

Mayer-Whittington, Nancy. *For the Love of Angela.* Indianapolis, IN: Saint Catherine of Siena Press, 2007. Print.

McCarter, Melissa Miles, ed. *Joy, Interrupted: An Anthology on Motherhood and Loss.* Ironton, MO: Fat Daddy's Press, 2013. Print.

McCracken, Elizabeth. *An Exact Replica of a Figment of My Imagination.* New York, NY: Back Bay Books/Little, Brown and Company, 2010. Print.

Miller, Angela. "Grateful and Grieving." *Still Standing Magazine,* 27 Nov. 2013. Web. 23 Nov. 2015.

"Miscarriage: Signs, Symptoms, Treatment and Prevention." AmericanPregnancy.org. American Pregnancy Association, August 2015. Web. 27 February 2016.

Nhat Hanh, Thich. *The Miracle of Mindfulness.* Boston, MA: Beacon Press, 1975. Print.

Nun Gavrilia. *The Ascetic of Love: Mother Gavrilia 2.10.1897–28.3.1992.* Trans. Helen Anthony. Athens, Greece: Talanto, 2006. Print.

Oliver, Mary. *House of Light.* Boston, MA: Beacon Press, 1990. Print.

The Paschal Service. Prepared by John Erickson and Very Reverend Paul Lazor. Wayne, NJ: Orthodox Christian Publications Center: n.d. Print.

Robins, Natalie. *Copeland's Cure: Homeopathy and the War Between Conventional and Alternative Medicine.* New York, NY: Alfred A. Knopf, 2005. Print.

Salzberg, Sharon, and Robert Thurman. "Embracing Our Enemies and Our Suffering." *On Being* podcast: On Being with Krista Tippett, 1 Jan. 2015. Web.

Schroedel, Jenny. *Naming the Child: Hope-filled Reflections on Miscarriage, Stillbirth, and Infant Death.* Brewster, MA: Paraclete Press, 2009. Print.

"Stillbirth: Trying to Understand." AmericanPregnancy.org. American Pregnancy Association, August 2015. Web. 27 February 2016.

Valentine, Jean. *The River at Wolf.* Cambridge, MA: Alice James Books, 1992. Print.

Vanier, Jean. "The Wisdom of Tenderness." *On Being*: On Being with Krista Tippett, 28 May 2015. Web.

Yacaboni, Celeste, ed. *How Do You Pray? Inspiring Responses from Religious Leaders, Spiritual Guides, Healers, Activists & Other Lovers of Humanity.* Rhinebeck, NY: Monkfish Book Publishing, 2014. Print.

Young, Kevin, ed. *The Art of Losing: Poems of Grief & Healing.* New York, NY: Bloomsbury USA, 2010. Print.

Zucker, Rachel. *Eating in the Underworld.* Middletown, CT: Wesleyan University Press, 2003. Print.

Resources

Coffins (Newborn/Miscarriage)
Heaven's Gain Ministries
heavensgain.com

Greeting Cards for Pregnancy and Infant Loss
Pregnancy Loss Cards by Dr. Jessica Zucker
shop.drjessicazucker.com

Sindy L. Strosahl "Healing Companion" Cards
etsy.com/shop/sindyart

Grief Support
SHARE, Pregnancy and Infant Loss Support
nationalshare.org

Word Bird Delivers (program for young siblings)
wordbirddelivers.com

Photography for Infant Loss
Now I Lay Me Down to Sleep
nowilaymedowntosleep.org

Support for Parents Carrying to Term with Fatal Diagnoses
Isaiah's Promise
isaiahspromise.net

Still Birthday
stillbirthday.com

Support for Trisomy 18 and 13
Perinatal Hospice and Palliative Care
perinatalhospice.org

Support Organization for Trisomy 18, 13 and Related Disorders (SOFT)
trisomy.org

Trisomy 18 Foundation
trisomy18.org

Acknowledgments

MANY PEOPLE SUPPORTED ME on my pregnancy journey and in the writing of this book.

Thank you to my awesome therapist, Dr. Adele Ryan McDowell, for countless emails and prayers at all hours of the day and night throughout my pregnancy and the after-months of deep grief. You have taught me how to do the shaman's work and transmute the darkness into Light while feeling and processing the pain. Yes, my heart is as broken and open as can be.

To Aniela Costello for her healing love and homeopathic and spiritual support throughout my pregnancy until this very day. You are an angel on earth helping us walk through the muck of pain and grief with Love.

To my birth team: Midwife Grace, I would not have had my home birth without your patient and loving care. You tenderly walked each step alongside me, showing great love for Mary Rose. Thank you for your many gifts, especially your calm wisdom in the middle of many stormy days. Midwife Elizabeth, thank you for opening your heart to my daughter. I am grateful for your presence and for your brother's blessings on this journey. Midwife Gloria Miles, thank you for blessing my pregnancy. Leslie Cuffee, Bereavement Doula, thank you for holding my still baby and for counting her among the ancestors. Sindy L. Strosahl, your painting, "Healing Companion," has touched many lives. Thank you for giving me the gift of birth photographs and friendship. Dr. Bina Fenn, you were key to our home-birth. Thank you for coming to our home to care for our daughter when no else would.

To Father John and Matushka Sunny Cox, you will always be an integral part of Mary Rose's short life. To the parishioners of the parish Dormition of the Theotokos in Norfolk, Virginia, who read the psalms over Mary Rose's body when I could not be there after labor: Susanna and Kristofer Carlson, Meg Downing, Paula and Arcel Dullas, Joy and James Messimer, Yana Lowry and the others who sang at Mary Rose's funeral and prayed for her.

Thank you Leslie Alvarado, Harriet Andronikides, Mary and George Andronikides, Missy Hilzendeger Axt, Judith Baumel, Dr. Alice Bell, Pat Bolger, Amber Kuileimailani Bonnici, Mary and Lee Buck, Mary Burgess, Elizabeth Carman, Renea Cicero, Father David and Matushka Tamara Cowan; Patty DeAngelis, Annmarie DiRado, Shalome Doran, Pattie Sandidge Dortch, Heidi Faith, Dr. Tiffany Fernandez, Dr. Jonathan Fleenor, Amy Wright Glenn, Raizy Goldsmith, Mariah Gonzalez-Outlaw, Christa Hall, Nancy Halseide, Elizabeth Harper, Gil

Hedley, Karen Hedley, Vicki Hedley, Joanna Clapps Herman, Terry Jones-Brady, Jane Johnson, Mary Potter Kenyon, Dr. Jamil Khan, Dan LaHood, Mary Frances LaHood, Thea Koula Lamanis, Lakshmi Light, Kathryn Los, Joanne and Paul Loutraris, Spiridoula and Dennis Louth, Shiloh Sophia McCloud, Isabel Buck McEachern, Anni McLaughlin, Debra Marino, Nancy Eagle Spirit Woman Martinez, Greg Mason, Robin Mayer, Nancy Mayer-Whittington, Marianela Medrano, Victoria J. Miller, Jennifer Gurdak Napolitano, Cathleen O'Connor, Elizabeth O'Hara, Dr. Emily O'Rourke, Dr. Ginger Oringer, Krissy Louth Orlen, Maria and Nick Papadoulias, Pourakis Family, especially Presbytera Georgia; Father James and Khouria Kelly Purdie; Dr. Sherry Reiter, Kirsty Reyes, Ann-Marie Richards, Laura C. Robb, Nicholas Samaras, Lauren Sample, Meghan Scam, Jeannie Smith, Sherri Snider, Miko Taylor, Lucy Allen Tenenbaum, Ruthie Tenenbaum, Jan Tritten, Judy and Steve Vandervelden, Barbara VanIerreweghe, Dianalee Velie, Westminster Presbyterian MOPS including Wendy Catt, Grace Cheely, Heather Dess, Lena Gopi, Lisa Hill and Holly Cooper McNeal; Maureen Winzig and Dr. Jessica Zucker.

To my adopted aunts, my dear Matina's closest friends, Vivian Kalogeras Anemoyanis (and the immortal Pauline), Joanna Bakatsias, Marika Drakos, Josephine Leonardelli, Louisa (Madame) Mason, Vita Santoro and Giovanna Saraceni.

To my closest friends from my time in Connecticut, Paige Bossi Fano, Lavinia Jennings, Brenda Peterson, Daniela Ragusa (and the immortal Laura) and Shari Specland. Thank you Father Vladimir and Matushka Suzanne Aleandro and the Christ the Savior community in Southbury for your prayers and love for over a decade.

To my longest friend, Rachel Kershenbaum Smith, and her parents Rabbi Peg and Aaron Kershenbaum for continuing to be lights in my life. Thank you for supporting this work.

To Sister Evelyn, Mother Maureen and all the sisters of Mount St. Mary's Abbey; Mother Raphaela and the nuns of Holy Myrrhbearers Monastery; the nuns of Holy Transfiguration Monastery, and the parish of the Orthodox Christian Church of the Holy Transfiguration in Pearl River, New York, thank you for your prayers and love.

To the midwives of this book and my website: White Flowers Press, publisher; Rosana Caffarena for design of the cover and heavenly garden graphic; Max Mitchell, web designer. Thank you to the readers of this manuscript especially Renea Cicero, Annie Consolvo, Aniela Costello, Terry Jones-Brady, Vivian Kalogeras Anemoyanis, Mary Frances LaHood, Anni McLaughlin, Joy Messimer, Daniela Ragusa and Stefanie Strathmann.

Annie Consolvo, you are a part of our family. Thank you for witnessing my pregnancy with Mary Rose, and for being present for her brief life.

To my dear aunt Evangelia Sarris, and my cousins Sophia and Ioanna, and all my family in Greece.

To my sister, Stefanie, and my brother-in-law, Timm, thank you for coming to Virginia, for attempting to meet Mary Rose even though you were about to look for a new home in a new state. Thank you Timm for driving your family from Illinois, flying back for work, and then back again to drive them home. For my godchildren, thank you for being awesome cousins to Mary Rose and my son.

To my parents, who love their children unconditionally. Thank you, Mother, for leaving work to tend to us all summer. Thank you for holding Mary Rose. Thank you, Daddy, for staying alone that difficult summer, and for coming to be with us. Even though you were not here for the birth, you met Mary Rose when I was pregnant.

A special thank you to Pat Walter and all the volunteers of Isaiah's Promise, who sew and knit and make packages and pray for their families with such love. Each gift that I received was treasured, and, more than the gifts, which acknowledged our daughter's life and gave us permission to be sorrowfully joyous about our daughter's birth, your prayers continue to change our lives.

To those who prayed and hoped and loved, though I do not know many of your names, thank you. And to my readers of my blog, thank you for opening your hearts to Mary Rose.

To the ancestors of Light, especially Despinaki, Matinaki, Mary Rose and Cubby, who were so close as I wrote this book. And Mother Mary who continues to hold me so close to her heart. . . .

Finally to my son who changed my life unexpectedly and quickly, you give me hope and love. And to my Sweet Man, Tim Armentrout, I'm so glad that we met at St. Paul's Cathedral one May afternoon. You turned my life right side up. Thank you for giving me my four children, our beloved living son, our daughter, Mary Rose, and our two miscarried babies. I am grateful for your love and support, which is real and true.

I am blessed.

About the Author

DIANNA VAGIANOS ARMENTROUT is a published writer, teacher, workshop facilitator and poetry therapist. She graduated from Adelphi University's Honors Program and earned her MAW from Manhattanville College. Dianna's pregnancy with her daughter, Mary Rose, who died an hour after birth of trisomy 18, changed her life completely. Her blog, *Walking the Labyrinth of My Heart*, was launched in April 2015 as a way of offering support to others going through pregnancies with difficult and fatal diagnoses.

Dianna wishes to change the cultural fear of death and social awkwardness around the bereaved by educating others to be present and open to the natural process of death. Not knowing what to say is fine. Let's sit together quietly not knowing what to say about our most difficult and sacred losses, because a loving community is vital to the healing of the bereaved in our broken world. Dianna volunteers with Isaiah's Promise as a peer minister, and can't help sending "Healing Companion" cards to mothers facing pregnancy and newborn losses.

She lives near the Great Dismal Swamp with her family, but has been feeling the call to go west. When she isn't writing or reading, she spends her time outdoors walking and gardening. Dianna also tinkers with recipes for paleo cookies and shares them with those around her.

Contact Dianna at www.diannavagianos.com or labyrinthofmyheart@gmail.com.